WHAT EVERY
CEO
MUST KNOW

37 SECRETS TO LEAD WITH
CONFIDENCE AND POWER

BILL MILLER

Praise for What Every CEO Must Know

Do you ever wish for an unredacted Reddit discussion room where other CEOs shared their blunders and lessons learned in order to shortcut your learning curve?

Well, you've found it in Bill Miller's *"What Every CEO Must Know"* because he relays the stories from the lips (or emails) of founders and CEOs to the page without trying to sugarcoat what went wrong.

It is as refreshing as it is useful for people at the top of the org chart as well as those who aspire to that role.

Once you have this book, study it, underline it, discuss it with your team, and implement the relevant ideas in your business. You'll find that the power of secrets comes not from their scarcity but from their execution. Learn from the experience, courage, and candor of these 24 CEOs to quickly advance your own leadership effectiveness.

— **Bill Ringle, 3X founder, 4X author, Finish Strong Friday leader for tech execs, and host of "My Quest for the Best," the podcast for ambitious SME leaders.**

Lead Smarter. Avoid Pitfalls. Accelerate Success.

In *What Every CEO Must Know, 37 CEO Secrets to Lead with Confidence and Power*, Bill Miller shares hard-earned lessons from real founders and executives who've faced the toughest leadership challenges and emerged stronger. These concise, actionable insights help you sidestep costly mistakes, recover quickly when setbacks strike, and build the clarity, confidence, and trust every leader needs.

-- **Endorsed by Rich Tehrani,** tech thought leader, CEO and Group Editor-in-Chief at TMC, founder of ITEXPO, and an investment banker, this book delivers a proven playbook for thriving as a CEO at any stage, from startup to enterprise.

The Ultimate CEO Playbook - Built from the Trenches.

What Every CEO Must Know isn't theory, it's raw, real-world wisdom from over 30 years in the leadership arena. Bill Miller distills 37 powerful lessons from seasoned founders, battle-tested executives, and resilient CEOs who have faced the fire and emerged stronger.

Each short, punchy chapter unpacks a mistake, a recovery, and a hard-won leadership secret. From vision and strategy to people, culture, ethics, crisis, and M&A, this book delivers what other leadership guides miss: **the truth behind the title.**

Whether you're a first-time founder or a veteran exec, these stories will save you scars, sharpen your instincts, and fuel your journey to confident, powerful leadership.

-- Dr. Timo Sandritter, Founder, RippleWorx (Acquired 2024)

In *What Every CEO Must Know*, Bill Miller distills critical lessons directly from the trenches. Having contributed my own story of leadership 'screw-ups' and growth, I can attest this isn't theory...it's the raw, actionable wisdom every leader needs. It uniquely exposes blind spots and provides playbooks to lead with confidence. A definitive resource for founders and CEOs ready to face hard truths and build lasting success.

-- Kevin Gaither, CEO of InsideSalesExpert.com and author of "It Happened On The Sales Floor: 100 Sensational Stories about Sales Leadership Screw-Ups and Big Wins"

I had the privilege of working alongside Bill as we navigated a tough, yet exciting period of technology growth. Bill is a rarity in his understanding of the human dynamics of "getting things done". I am happy to share my learnings with him in hope others can benefit from lessons learned.

-- Gary Lee, CEO and Board Member of B2M Solutions

ISBN: 978-1-7356538-4-6 (Paperback)
ISBN: 978-1-7356538-5-3 (Hardcover)
ISBN: 978-1-7356538-3-9 (eBook)

Book Cover Design and Interior Formatting by 100Covers.

Dedications

Dedicated to all CEOs I worked for, all CEOs who are my clients, all my non-CEO clients, all CEOs who worked with me over the years and became founders and CEOs, and every leader who aspires to become a founder and/or CEO.

And, of course, I dedicate this book to my fiancée, Connie Lund, who provides ongoing support for my passion of helping people, especially first-time CEOs, and her clients from her Growth Rebel program.

Free Offer Bonus

As a thank you for purchasing my book, I am offering my updated "7 Tips for the Rookie CEO" and several editable frameworks for you. These have been updated with content from this book, *What Every CEO Must Know, 37 Secrets to Lead With Confidence and Power*

Email me at *bill@billmillertheCEOguy.com* and write "7 Tips" in the subject line. These tips are not offered anywhere else, and are exclusively for you, the purchaser of my books.

Initially, these frameworks and checklists are included each as one-page downloadable and editable Excel sheets.

1. Leadership Operating System Guide

2. Non-Negotiable Leadership Principles Checklist

3. Culture Framework Guide

4. CEO Forward Plan, a Quarterly Priority Checklist

These valuable tips are rooted in my personal experiences of 50 years in the trenches, and the past 35+ years as a senior executive. You will learn from these tips and frameworks and be able to insert them into your leadership life immediately.

Table of Contents

What Every CEO Must Know, 37 CEO Secrets to Lead With Confidence and Power is an essential resource guide for CEOs and leaders that helps them to avoid pitfalls and providing strategies for recovery and success.

Preface

Why I Wrote This Book

At this stage of my career, my mission is clear: help CEOs avoid the costly mistakes I've seen and made over 35+ years in leadership. I've been a senior executive and a coach, and I'm now an advisor to founders, first-time CEOs, and operators at every stage. What you'll find in these pages is not theory, it's hard-won wisdom from the trenches.

The CEOs in this book range from early-stage founders to leaders of global companies. What they share is authenticity. Each story reveals the decisions, tension, and consequences behind closed doors. You'll learn not just what went wrong, but how the CEOs recovered, what they'd do differently, and what they wish they'd known earlier.

There are many books on leadership. But *What Every CEO Must Know* fills a crucial gap. It offers real-world case studies, not theories, from leaders who may not be household names, but whose insights are gold for any CEO who wants to succeed with fewer scars.

Whether you're preparing for your first CEO role or leading a fast-growing company, this book is your roadmap to leading with confidence and power, one story at a time.

In some of the stories in the book, I am an integral part of the story. Welcome to *What Every CEO Must Know, 37 CEO Secrets to Lead With Confidence and Power!*

Introduction

What Makes This Book Different

If you're reading this, you've either made leadership mistakes or want to avoid them. Good. That's where leadership begins.

This isn't a memoir. It's not a theory book. It's a practical collection of true CEO stories that are short, honest, and immediately useful. Most of the leaders featured here are still in the game. Some are scaling their next venture to new levels of success. A few are rebuilding. But all are generous enough to share their lessons, so you don't repeat them in your journey.

Each chapter follows a simple pattern:

    1. What happened

    2. Why it happened

    3. What the CEO learned

    4. How they recovered

    5. The "secret" you can use

The chapters are grouped by theme: strategy, communication, decision-making, ethics, people leadership, and startup challenges. You can read them front to back or jump to what you need most in your situation. Every chapter stands on its own.

Why it matters:

The smallest blind spot can jeopardize the biggest vision. This book helps you recognize those moments, respond with clarity, and lead through the storm with confidence.

You'll walk away with:

- Stories that mirror your current challenges.

- Playbooks and frameworks that reduce risk.

- Tools to lead with more confidence, speed, and resilience.

And, perhaps most importantly, the reassurance that even great CEOs stumble. The best ones just recover faster.

So, let's get into it. Mistakes are coming. Secrets are waiting. It's time to become the confident, powerful CEO you were meant to be.

Acknowledgements

A special thank you to all CEOs who worked with me and provided the stories in the book. These CEOs provided their mistake, how the mistake happened, details about the blunder, the results, and how they recovered. I am especially grateful that these CEOs were authentic, open, and willing to share with the common goal of helping other CEOs and leaders:

Rob Black

Kevin Gaither

Dave George

Jody Gonzales

Adam Helweh

Gary Lee

Tony Lewis

Bill McClain

Jonathan Reeves

Mike Williams

CEOs from my book, *The Rookie CEO, You Can't Make This Stuff Up!*:

The Cyclone

The Dealmaker

The Flyboy

The General

The Opportunist

Thank you to all CEOs who agreed to be identified only by their first name and wanted to provide their story for the purpose of educating and enlightening others. Full names and companies are protected since these CEOs are still active and chose to stay anonymous. These include:

Bob

Greg

Lexi

Lubdo

Mark

Robert

Sean

Tom

Part 1
Strategic Lessons

Chapter 1

The Cost of Losing Sight: A Serial CEO's Hard Life Lesson

Dave George, the CEO of GreenStar Marketing and a serial entrepreneur, learned a painful lesson in leadership and life balance. His career mistake (and what he learned from it) wasn't about strategy, markets, or operations, but it was about something far more personal and often overlooked by many CEOs: the toll that unchecked passion for business can take on relationships and personal well-being. Business gratification is no match for your loved ones' gratification (family)! Business success has its dangers related to your family, health, and heart!

Make sure you truly want to become a CEO, if that is your dream or current situation! If this is your path, be better prepared as you will learn in this book. This is easy to say but tougher to execute.

The Mistake

Dave's biggest mistake was letting his passion for his business consume him, to the point that it damaged relationships he only came to fully appreciate after they were already fractured. He admits that, in the moment, he couldn't see the harm his single-minded focus was causing. "If I'm busy and successful, and I'm getting recognition, I must be doing the right things," he thought. But, as the demands of leadership piled up, so did the hidden costs.

The gratification Dave got from his business: the wins, the growth, and the recognition, couldn't replace the deep satisfaction of meaningful connections with loved ones. His business accomplishments don't make up for family moments he missed. This is the core of his regret: in pursuing success, he sacrificed relationships that truly mattered.

How He Could Have Avoided It

Dave candidly admits that, at the time, he could have avoided the mistake if he had simply recognized it as a problem. These are unseen elements that others can observe and are your blind spots. Like many young founders and CEOs, Dave was navigating a steep learning curve. He was proud of his hard work and achievements, but overconfidence clouded his ability to see that work alone wouldn't solve all his problems.

There's a fine line between taking pride in your accomplishments and letting that pride distance you from the people who matter most. The imbalance Dave experienced affected both the business and his family.

In hindsight, Dave acknowledges the importance of work and life balance. He learned that, when loved ones raise concerns about your focus, they often signal that they care and need you. It's easy to fall into the trap of making business your life's priority, but Dave now knows he should have been more intentional about prioritizing his family and friends. It was easy to get caught up in your successful business. Taking breaks wouldn't have hurt his company. In fact, he believes it might have recharged him and made him a better CEO.

The takeaway? Pay attention to those around you. If your loved ones are signaling that you're overdoing it, listen. Make time for them, and don't assume that continuing to grind away at your business challenges will solve every issue.

The Recovery

When asked how he recovered, Dave's answer is raw and honest: he didn't, not fully. The damage was done. He didn't regain what was lost but instead moved on, taking the lessons he learned to his next venture. Dave's recovery was less about fixing what had already happened and more about reshaping his approach to leadership and personal relationships going forward.

A Quote From Dave

Dave has stated, "And it has struck me lately, having played my part as both a founder and CEO several times over, that the simple knack of knowing who you are, and being okay with it, and being that person every single moment, without pause, is a surprisingly rare achievement. Maybe it only comes with age. Several decades worth. Or maybe a few people are just born with a gift for it, this innate ability for being able to balance it all out day one. Who knows? But, for me, I'll keep learning, improving, trying."

What stands out in Dave's reflection is the vulnerability he embraced along the way. He sought help, embraced counseling, and leveraged his network. He learned to be an expert at self-awareness.

As he became more self-aware, his emotional intelligence (EQ) blossomed, and he now recognizes this as essential to leadership.

How He Moved Forward

Dave's journey forward is an ongoing process. Dave now recognizes that emotional intelligence is important and checks in with himself on a regular basis to stay attuned.

He's still learning and still growing, but now he's more vigilant. He actively makes a conscious effort to maintain work-life balance. One of the biggest challenges for him has been transitioning from a founder's mindset to that of a CEO. As a founder, he felt a deep connection to every part of the business, but to scale, he had to learn to delegate, trust his team, and focus on growing the company rather than getting lost in the day-to-day. We will address more on delegation later with other CEOs.

The shift from founder to CEO didn't happen overnight for Dave. It's still a work in progress. He's come to realize that, while sprinting is part of the job, it's not a sustainable pace. Living in constant overdrive puts more than his health at risk; it strains relationships and can even jeopardize the company itself.

Like many founders, Dave sees his startup as his "child," something he's poured himself into, nurtured, and fought to grow.

These days, he's more intentional about staying connected to his family and friends. That grounding keeps him balanced.

Conclusion

Dave George's experience is not unique. These are common challenges many CEOs experience. Learn from Dave that business, even your prized startup, can't replace the love and support of those closest to you.

CEOs, especially first-time founders, must be mindful of the risks of overcommitting to the business at the expense of personal relationships and well-being.

First-time founders and, really, any CEO need to be aware of the cost that comes from giving everything to the business while neglecting their own well-being and relationships. That trade-off may feel necessary in the moment, but it rarely ends well.

Secret #1: Pay attention to the people who care about you. Step away when you need to. Balance isn't a luxury; it's how you stay in the game. Revenue may rise and fall, but the time, laughter, and love you share with family and friends are the things that truly last.

Chapter 2

Vision and Strategy

All CEOs own the company vision supported by the strategy. Vision is what the company wants to become (your "why"), and the strategy is how you, as CEO, will guide the company there (your "how").

The Mistake

Not all first-time CEOs are equipped to lead both direction-setting roles. Some longer-term CEOs have gaps in their skill sets for these roles but hire a second-in-command leader to head up at least one of these roles, usually strategy.

These gaps cause blind spots in their experience, which is why hiring either a cofounder or new senior executive with these complementary skills becomes important.

Lacking trusted partners is one of the most typical mistakes CEOs make, especially first-timers or any CEO in today's world of artificial intelligence, where new products and web-based tools may be created by AI, which become SaaS (software as a service) offerings, where the founder/CEO brings little to no experience in the market.

How to Avoid This Mistake

A strong and experienced advisor, coach, or mentor can provide this role as a contractor or on a fractional basis to guide you through their go-to-market phase.

Using this method can save equity and dollars helping the cap table (capitalization table) and the cash flow. An important business value to you, when you have an outside coach or advisor, is you can talk to them about anything without jeopardizing your leadership to someone on your team.

The Architectologist, whose story you will read later, has shared how he has his inside number two for working through company issues, but he utilizes an advisor for his personal CEO challenges on a regular basis. Jody has shared the business and personal value she has gained from an outside coach as well.

How to Recover

Your executive team provides leadership, while your advisor or coach provides perspective.

Unlike many of the generic startup and CEO books that gloss over this: not having a trusted partner in vision and strategy is a top reason CEOs either hit a brick wall or get replaced.

In a perfect world, hire your number two executive and hire an advisor, mentor or coach.

Moving Forward

How do you know when this is not a problem? You have a primary Plan A where you know exactly what you are developing, testing, and bringing to market. Your Go-To-Market Plan is solid. As you will see in Gary Lee's story, you need a Plan B and maybe a Plan C, in case there are breakdowns, especially in markets that can change rapidly.

Conclusion

Do a thirty-second self-test. Ask yourself right now:

If Plan A falls apart next quarter, do I have an idea for Plan B? Or will I have to panic?

You can easily prevent new blind spots by applying this chapter's secret.

Secret #2: As founder, first-time CEO, or serial CEO, you need a number two. It might be a cofounder, an outside coach, or a senior executive leader on your team. The title does not matter. The trust does!

Chapter 3

The Over-confidence of Your Plan A

Gary Lee is a six-time founder/CEO and seasoned entrepreneur who has consistently steered his startups to success. But, with one startup that he believed had the biggest upside, he learned the hard way what happens when you bet it all on one perfect outcome.

The danger wasn't inexperience. It was success. After successfully growing the company from idea to market growth in the United States, United Kingdom, Asia Pacific, and in the European Union, Gary believed he could see around every corner. But over-confidence, especially the kind that comes from winning, can be just as blinding as naiveté.

Background

Gary's company was on a tear. Growth was strong. The team was firing on all cylinders. Investors were talking IPO, and the timing looked perfect. The markets were favorable for his company. The bankers were enthusiastic. Momentum was real.

Then, a large European company came calling with a serious acquisition offer. Prestigious name, solid terms. It seemed like the dream scenario: a hot market for an IPO or a strong potential acquisition.

Either outcome would mean a massive win for the team and the investors. So, Gary and his team poured everything into making one of those two options a reality.

Everything became focused on Plan A.

The Mistake

What Gary didn't see coming was how quickly market conditions could turn. The public markets started to wobble. Investor confidence slipped. The IPO was shelved.

Then, just as they were finalizing the acquisition, the deal fell apart, literally the day before approval.

Now Gary had no IPO, no acquisition, and no backup plan. The team had built toward one vision and one exit. But, without a Plan B, or C or D, they were stuck. Panic time.

The mistake wasn't ambition. It was putting everything on a single path and assuming it would go according to plan. It was over-confidence disguised as conviction.

"Why do most CEOs avoid Plan B?" Gary asked me later. "Because Plan A is exciting. Plan B feels like failure. But if you're only planning for Plan A, you're not leading, you're just hoping."

The Result

The board told Gary to freeze spending, cut staff, and preserve cash. Almost overnight, the company went from a lucrative exit track to survival mode.

Eventually, the company was sold but at a steep discount. It was a painful exit that didn't reflect the company's potential. Most of the team was laid off. Several years of hard work and tremendous hope were lost.

For Gary, it was gutting. What started as his most promising venture ended in a way he never expected. The emotional weight was real. He had seen success before, but this was a heart-wrenching reminder that even the best plans can fall apart, and fast.

How to Avoid This Mistake

Gary's story is a lesson in contingency planning. CEOs can't afford to be one-plan leaders. The world doesn't care how great your idea is. The market shifts. Deals stall. Competitors emerge. Cash dries up. Deals fall apart.

Gary now swears by having multiple paths ready. His personal checklist for preventing this blind spot includes:

- Hold quarterly business reviews with scenario planning baked in.

- Review every aspect of your business, across business functions including sales, marketing, finance, operations, and legal for vulnerabilities.

- Identify top risks across funding, customer retention, and product roadmap.

- Document two to three fallback strategies and assign clear ownership.

- Build these backup plans while things are going well, not when you're already in trouble.

Contingency planning isn't pessimism. It's leadership.

Recovery

Gary didn't bounce back overnight. There was no dramatic comeback. The loss stayed with him. But it shaped him and made him better.

He leads differently now. He's more measured, more deliberate. He's still confident but always scanning for risks. He builds optionality into every big move. He's always ready if the market shifts, the deal stalls, or the runway shortens.

Today, Gary is a respected leader with the kind of experience people trust. His approach is grounded, practical, and shaped by what he's lived through.

Conclusion

Gary's story reminds us: Success can dull your edge if you stop questioning your assumptions. Confidence is good, but without backup plans, it can turn into a trap.

Even the most experienced CEOs need to stay sharp, humble, and ready.

Secret #3: If your only plan must work, it probably won't. The CEOs who survive are the ones who build options early so they can pivot fast and zig when the market zags.

Chapter 4

Dishonest Competitors

The Flyboy (introduced in *The Rookie CEO: You Can't Make This Stuff Up!* book), a rising young CEO star, was winning until a competitor claimed they had written and owned Flyboy's core software. People believed it.

The Mistake

Flyboy had not been paying detailed attention to this competitor, even though both participated in the same tradeshows and conferences. The competitor had created a chart on his website that put Flyboy's company down vs. his company in a chart.

Flyboy didn't just miss the competitor's attack. He underestimated how fast that false information could spread in a distracted market, and how slow the truth would be to catch up.

Even worse, the chart was wrong, but customers didn't know this fact unless they tested each product and compared them. They saved time and skipped over this level of due diligence and often bought the competitor's solution. This became a serious problem.

Setting the Stage

When you are a young, maybe an under-thirty first-time founder CEO, you still must be aware of not only yourself, but of all your surroundings in the market, or you can be sideswiped. Things that you can't see, but everyone around you can, are your blind spots. Learning how to recognize your blind spots and work through them is a critical CEO success factor.

Flyboy was preoccupied by raising venture funds, hiring and expanding his company, and traveling. He was involved in nearly everything. But this one got through him, and he was not listening.

The Decision Process

On a trip to visit a major prospective global customer with his senior leadership team, Flyboy's attention finally shifted. Mid-flight, his number two executive had his undivided attention showing the competitor's false claims. With time to think, he reviewed the document of the competitor's comparison chart. The claims were outrageous: false statements, misleading comparisons, and even an assertion that the competitor had written and owned Flyboy's core software.

The evidence was impossible to ignore. Flyboy's frustration hit hard. What started as disbelief turned into urgency. By the time the plane landed, he had committed to a new plan.

The Results

Back at the office, Flyboy and his team went on the offensive in a professional manner. They launched a fact-based PR response and worked their networks to correct the narrative. The goal wasn't drama; it was credibility.

At the next trade show, the competitor's CEO heard the message loud and clear. Their false claims and misleading charts were taken down after being warned of legal consequences.

The damage wasn't permanent, but the lesson was unforgettable: staying blind to competitor activity, even while focused on growth, comes at a cost.

How to Avoid This Mistake

You need to stay self-aware and fully aware of your surroundings in the marketplace. Listen to your sales team, product team, and any other person who provides feedback to you about your competitors. Feedback is how you eliminate blind spots that others see.

This type of motion and activity will prevent and help you manage this type of threat against you and your company.

Recovery and Moving Forward

Once the competitor, who had now been called out, changed his story and website chart, there was a renewed energy to watch all competitors more closely. This type of competitive situation does occur in various markets where there are multiple players and market share battles, and position is highly valuable.

Conclusion

In this simple case, there was pain and Flyboy was upset, but once he realized he needed to stay self-aware and market-aware, he was more confident and powerful as a leader. As CEO, be relentless in this activity and approach!

Here is a suggested market monitoring checklist for your company:

1. Designate a competitive "lead" on your team.

2. Create alerts for your competitors, and track tradeshows, startup, and funding announcements.

3. Hold a weekly or monthly "competitive analysis" lunch that includes key team members from sales, product, and support, and compare everything from rumors to "I heard" from prospects, LinkedIn posts,

and other channels to keep a competitive landscape map.

4. Schedule quarterly "deep dives" on those with whom your sales team or channel is competing with. Include website reviews, messaging, ads, and anything else you can find.

5. Create programs to compete in channels and messaging for web, tradeshows, PR, etc.

6. Keep the legal department abreast when dishonest players arise.

You will be glad you did! You will become more confident and powerful!

Secret #4: Be self-aware and fully market-aware of your surroundings in the marketplace. It will prevent blind spots and help you manage dishonest competitors.

Chapter 5

When Pride Meets Principle: The Rise and Fall of Seek Local, Inc.

The entrepreneurial journey often requires a blend of innovation, perseverance, and sometimes, a strong dose of humility. For Tony Lewis, the cofounder of Seek Local, Inc., these ingredients were in play, but one crucial misstep turned a promising venture into an experience like none other.

The Birth of Seek Local, Inc.

Today, Tony Lewis is cofounder and CEO of Clearly IP, and he shares his story from his days as cofounder and president of Seek Local, Inc. His story exemplifies the types of challenges CEOs and founders might face today and highlights how younger generations with less professional experiences might stumble. Pay attention to the learnings from this simple yet difficult challenge Tony faced.

In 2006, Tony was at the helm of an exterior modeling business with offices in two states, five locations, and a team of hundreds of employees and contractors. The company was thriving, yet Tony saw an opportunity to break into a different market, one that seemed ripe for disruption.

The idea for Seek Local, Inc. was simple yet powerful. At that time, the Yellow Pages was still a dominant force in local advertising, especially in markets like Appleton, Oshkosh, and Green Bay, Wisconsin. Each of these cities had its own phone book, and local businesses were forced to spend significant amounts of money to advertise in all three. The inefficiency was glaring, and Tony, along with his partner, believed they had a solution: one phone book to cover all three markets, offering a more comprehensive and cost-effective option for local businesses.

On top of that, they planned to revolutionize the way advertising fees were structured. Instead of charging businesses large sums of money for ad space, Seek Local would charge a nominal fee for the ad and then bill businesses based on the number of calls generated from each ad. It was a forward-thinking model, one that anticipated the pay-for-performance trends that would later dominate online advertising.

Tony hired a local retired forty-year anchor weatherman from the Green Bay market to be a company spokesman. People loved this on-air personality. This brought credibility to Seek Local. This single move changed the company trajectory in year one. They were on their way!

The Mistake That Cost It All

Tony's downfall came not from a lack of vision but from a surplus of ego and pride. The Telecom Act of 1996 mandated that Regional Bell Operating Companies (RBOCs) like Ameritech (later AT&T) sell residential listings to independent phone book companies like Seek Local. But when Tony's team approached Ameritech for the listings, they were met with resistance. Ameritech responded with a contract filled with unreasonable demands, including indemnification clauses and a multi-million-dollar bond that no startup could realistically afford.

Rather than acquiesce, Tony chose to fight. His legal team, bolstered by the confidence of a young, successful entrepreneur, decided to take on AT&T in federal court. The decision to stand on principle, to "stick it to" Ameritech, would prove to be a costly one.

The legal battle was intense. Ameritech arrived in court with an army of attorneys, dwarfing Tony's modest team. The court initially denied their injunction, prolonging the case and delaying Seek Local's ability to launch its phone book. By the time they won the case, the damage was done. They had to resort to purchasing a third-party list of residential numbers while they battled Ameritech in court. This data turned out to be outdated and inaccurate. The result was tens of thousands of complaints from customers, tarnishing the reputation of a company that had barely gotten off the ground.

The Legal Battle Setup

Tony believed deeply in what he was building. The Seek Local model was sound, customers responded, and momentum was real. However, access to Ameritech's residential phone listings was the final piece that determined the company's ability to execute the plan as envisioned.

That's when the real fight began.

Ameritech, the local telecom Goliath, responded with a contract packed with impossible terms: multi-million-dollar bonds, sweeping indemnification clauses, and bureaucratic hurdles no young company could reasonably clear. For Tony, it felt personal, like the system was rigged against innovation. He saw their demands as an insult and a threat to everything he had built.

The easy move? Sign the deal, get the listings, publish the phonebook, and live to fight another day. But that wasn't who Tony was at age twenty-six. With success from his first business under his belt and the wind of a new venture at his back, compromise looked too much like surrender.

He chose to fight.

Tony's legal team was small but confident. They filed in federal court, prepared to challenge Ameritech head-on. On the other side, Ameritech arrived with an army of attorneys. It was David vs. Goliath, but the slingshot doesn't always win in federal court.

While the case dragged on, Seek Local had no choice but to move forward. They purchased a third-party list to stay on schedule, but the data was outdated, full of errors, and far from reliable. Thousands of complaints poured in, and credibility began to crumble before the business even had a chance to scale.

The Lessons Learned

Reflecting on this experience, Tony acknowledged that his ego, pride, and inexperience led him down the wrong path. At 26 years old, with one successful business under his belt, he believed he was invincible. But this mistake, allowing pride and principle to dictate business decisions, taught him a lesson he wouldn't ever forget.

In hindsight, Tony realized he should have accepted Ameritech's terms, at least for the first year, to get the phone book published and maintain momentum. He could have fought for better terms later, but the need to prove a point, to not back down, ultimately helped lead to the demise of Seek Local.

This chapter isn't just about Tony's mistake. It's about a universal truth in business: Sometimes, principles must be set aside for the greater good of the company. It's about recognizing when to fight and when to compromise, even when the terms seem unfair.

Recovery and Moving Forward

After the fall of Seek Local, Tony didn't sit still. He took the lessons from that experience and applied them to his other ventures. He continued to grow his exterior remodeling business and eventually found success in other areas after his successful exit from the remodeling industry. But he never forgot the sting of losing Seek Local, the first and only time he lost money in a business venture. In the years that followed, Tony founded or co-founded multiple technology companies, each with clear differentiation, got acquired as CEO and then led the larger organization applying his experiences from Seek Local.

He then cofounded his current company with trusted executives from his past roles.

For other CEOs, especially those new to the game (first-time or rookie CEOs), Tony's story provides powerful guidance: don't let pride and ego cloud your judgment. Know when to pick your battles, and understand that sometimes, the best decision is the one that keeps your company afloat, even if it means swallowing your pride.

Tony's journey also highlights the importance of focus. Splitting your attention between multiple ventures can lead to mistakes that might have been avoided if you were fully present in the business. It's a warning for any entrepreneur trying to juggle too many balls at once. His head was only part-time into Seek Local because he was also part-time in his remodeling business.

Conclusion

The fall of Seek Local, Inc. was a hard lesson in humility and the dangers of letting pride and ego drive decision-making. But, like all good stories, it's one that offers invaluable lessons. For any CEO reading this, take Tony's experience to heart. Know when to fight, but more importantly, know when to fold because, sometimes, the cost of winning can be more than your business can afford. This story and your takeaways from it are a strong guide to becoming a confident and powerful CEO and leader.

Secret #5: Don't let pride and ego cloud your judgment! The cost is high. This may be hard to do, because most CEOs have a higher level of pride, especially in their company. Hint: Ego feels like strength, but it's a trap. Pride can sink your company faster than a bad idea. Know when to lead with principle and when to let it go!

Our mission: Lead with confidence and power!

Chapter 6

Innovation Blind Spots: How Market Leaders Fall

Falling from market leadership hurts. Doing it twice? That's a gut punch.

In the mid-1980s, General DataComm (GDC) dominated the T1 multiplexer space with its Megamux product, holding over 35% market share. But two critical mistakes led to a decline that no marketing campaigns or clever strategy could fix.

This chapter takes you inside the boardroom to show what happens when a CEO ignores disruption and fails to adapt. For any CEO navigating today's AI-driven landscape, the lesson is timeless: innovation ignored is market share lost.

As a quick crash course, the Time Division Multiplexer (TDM) era was highly competitive and Timeplex, another key player, captured around 18% of the market that same year. This was long before IP Networking became mainstream. This was a period of significant growth in the sector, as the T1 multiplexer market doubled in size. GDC owned the space. But it was not enough to sustain market leadership. And it will not save you either if you are not watching disruption and competition all around your company and solutions.

There was a constant flow of new technology that caused continuous disruption in the networking industry, and this change was being noted in the industry by analysts.

Jonathan (Jon) Reeves, who is currently CEO of CSignum, a serial entrepreneur, and venture partner, was heading up the technology at GDC at the time working closely with Charles P Johnson (CPJ), CEO of GDC and quite a type-A eccentric leader. Jon was always in CPJ's ear about market dynamics and changes.

Mistake #1

This chapter spans twenty years and two major blind spots. Both were avoidable, preventable, and repeated!

GDC missed the transition away from T1 multiplexing toward new technologies known as fast packet technologies such as Frame Relay, SMDS, proprietary fast packet (Stratacom), and cell relay which later became known as

ATM (Asynchronous Transfer Mode). Jon was educating CPJ to invest.

The failure of CPJ to see this change early led to a major decline in market cap, layoffs, and morale issues.

By the mid-1990s, GDC earned a significant market share in the global Asynchronous Transfer Mode (ATM) edge switch market by acquiring a small technology-based UK company. Jon led this initiative. At its peak, GDC commanded **38% of the worldwide market**, positioning it as a dominant player in the space. This market was growing rapidly, and by 1995, GDC aimed to replicate this success in the fast-expanding Asian market, targeting a similar strategy through strategic partnerships. But wait.

Mistake #2

With ATM Access exploding onto the scene, and Jon pleading with CPJ to develop ATM access in-house, he refused to invest yet again. What happened next? Jon left GDC.

Jon's new startup company focused on this solution, which lowered the cost and increased the density for smaller regions and branch offices.

GDC was still growing on the switch side but was under attack from others and new companies appeared with lower cost ATM to ATM Access devices.

This second mistake was due to CPJ's not buying into the rapid innovation and change. Lightning struck twice as CPJ missed this market again.

Setting the stage

Cisco began acquiring startups to accelerate its transition to IP over Ethernet.

While Cisco did not have fully working solutions, the market believed in their direction and the shift away from ATM momentum began.

The Decision Process

In GDC's Mistake #1, TDM, CPJ simply missed the trend and underestimated new competitive pressures. The setback was costly. His belief in his strategy was short sighted and he did not listen to his team of leaders and advisors.

In GDC's Mistake #2, ATM Access, the opportunity was there, but CPJ chose to execute his own way which included internal competition from four different development teams in four locations to see who could bring a product to market faster. This was costly in time, money and lost market position.

During this time, senior leaders attended major global partner meetings that could have provided lucrative exit opportunities.

However, CPJ directed the team to not engage with potential partners unless he was guaranteed a board seat in any acquiring company's headquarters. This was a non-starter for potential partners, and these meetings which included one as far as Helsinki, Finland, resulted in no deals due to CPJ's demands.

The Results

The second mistake took GDC out of contention in larger global deals. Then it started to lose smaller deals. Eventually, GDC sold off three of four business units to avoid bankruptcy, keeping only one set of technology. Top leaders left the company which lost its way.

How to Avoid These Mistakes

These were both CEO mistakes. Top leaders told CPJ what to do and proposed solutions, only to be turned away by CPJ's know-it-all ego which took the company down.

Your CEO decisions should be based on listening, asking questions, being curious, and exploring. Your success may be at stake.

Here are some innovations-related blind spots to be aware of:

- Ignoring or delaying investment in emerging markets.

- Requiring control, before partner discussions (i.e. board seat).

- Blocking alternatives that could generate growth.

- Facilitating internal competition which can eliminate momentum.

- Complacency towards senior team warnings without reason or data.

Recovery and Moving Forward

The company still exists today, but as a tiny fraction of its former self. Once a global leader, GDC now picks up "crumbs" in older networks. They found a small application set their technology supported and continue to sell and service these networks today.

The overall market changed as well, as IP (Internet Protocol) became the internet as we know it today, based on IP routers. This is what GDC attempted to do with a partner. However, the leader, Cisco, was too fast and too wealthy for GDC to take advantage of this key trend.

Conclusion

As CEO, it is up to you to lead strategy and direction. But trust and challenge your leadership team to keep you abreast of trends your customers are addressing and getting behind.

Get out from behind your desk, visit customers and partners, attend conferences live, talk to your peers in CEO peer groups, utilize a coach/partner, build a "muscle" to keep your mindset alert of your current technology or solutions and where you might best expand and grow your business in existing and adjacent markets.

Secret #6: Innovation is not a threat; delaying adoption and investment is. Watch for innovation and change relentlessly. Map your strengths, weaknesses, opportunities, and threats (SWOT). Your leadership team and subject matter experts should be actively involved in keeping you abreast with market dynamics and threats and maintain an ongoing SWOT analysis. Hint: A CEO who stops listening and learning becomes the company's biggest risk.

Chapter 7

The Excitement and Speedbumps of an Acquisition

This is not a story about a bad deal. It is about what happens when leadership underestimates what comes *after* the deal closes.

In the world of business, acquisitions are often seen as a fast track to growth, innovation, and market expansion. But, as any seasoned executive will tell you, closing the deal is just the beginning. It's all about the integration of the two companies.

This chapter tells the story of a CEO, formerly a COO at a large public company, who faced the challenge of merging two companies with shared development visions. Acquisitions demand meticulous planning and due diligence, strong leadership, and, most importantly, experience in the art of M&A.

Background

The General, featured in, *The Rookie CEO: You Can't Make This Stuff Up!* was no stranger to the business. As a board member representing a major investor, he had insight, influence, and a front-row seat to the acquisition.

When he stepped into the CEO role, his confidence was high. He had helped negotiate the deal. He knew all the people involved. The due diligence team believed the cultures would mesh. The technical team was fired up. But the business team? They were cautious.

The technical team was enthusiastic. They loved the technology, respected the team, and believed the cultures would mesh perfectly. The business side, however, had reservations. But with the technical side's strong endorsement, the acquisition moved forward, and the General, armed with his board experience, felt ready to lead the integration efforts of the two companies.

The Mistake

The biggest mistake? The General assumed familiarity with the teams and the key players was the same as readiness to move forward and execute.

Instead of taking charge, the General let the acquired company operate like a separate entity. They kept their own email, company signage, and worse, its own culture. The former CEO of the acquired company later became a disruptor, undermining trust and resisting integration. He wanted a payout and spotlight, not accountability.

The sales and channel marketing teams of the acquiring company were thrilled with the new product and threw themselves into selling it. However, they ignored the broader integration efforts, leading to a fractured company identity. The acquired company's independence created a rift within the senior leadership team, exacerbating the challenges of integration.

The Result

Initially, the numbers looked promising. The product sold well, and there were moments of optimism. But these were overshadowed by the growing tensions. The former CEO of the acquired company became a thorn in most everyone's side, resisting the new direction and clashing with some executives from the acquiring company. The acquisition's strategic goals were lost in the infighting, and it took nearly three years for the full breakdown to occur.

Eventually, the disruptive former CEO was terminated but, by then, much of the damage had been done. It took time to recover.

How to Avoid This Mistake

This is an example of the importance of strong and powerful leadership in M&A integration. Hindsight being 20/20, the General could have taken charge from the beginning, setting a clear direction and leading the effort to integrate the acquired company into the larger organization. A cross-functional team, working closely with the acquired company's leadership, could have established a cohesive strategy and execution plan, ensuring joint buy-in and a unified approach. But this did not happen. It was fragmented from the initial celebration party.

In some acquisitions, it might make sense for the acquired company to operate as a wholly owned subsidiary, maintaining independence. But even in these cases, there needs to be a clear strategy for integration across business functions to gain economies of scale. In this instance, the piecemeal approach, integrating only those aspects the acquired company didn't care about, led to years of infighting and lost opportunities.

Recovery and Long-Term Impact

After years of missed opportunities, the General finally acted and made the difficult decision to change leadership and fully integrate the acquired company. However, the lost time and resources were significant, and the integration should never have taken so long. This experience taught the General, and those around him, that success in M&A is never guaranteed, no matter how promising the outlook or how well the cultures might appear to fit.

A new leader was hired to head up the acquired company. He worked closely with the parent company, the executive team, the sales team, and the integration vision was finally executed and progressing.

Conclusion

This chapter is a lesson in the perils of overconfidence and the dangers of underestimating the complexities of what looked like a simple acquisition. Even the most seasoned executives can find themselves struggling when it comes to integrating two companies with misaligned goals.

The key takeaway is clear: bring in an M&A advisor without skin in the game, who has been there before. Someone who can identify blind spots and provide the expertise needed to navigate the challenges of integration. With the right guidance and process, these costly mistakes can be avoided, ensuring that the promise of an acquisition can be fully realized. It is never easy, but experience can minimize mistakes.

Here is an adaptable integration readiness checklist:

- Create and follow an integration playbook.

- Name an integration executive lead and empower them.

- Determine Day One and Day Ninety communications plans and share.

- Talk to peer groups, a CEO coach, and an M&A advisor who has done this before.

Secret #7: The deal is not done when it is signed. Integration leverages where value is created or destroyed. Integration requires planning, leadership, and discipline exactly as the acquisition itself does. If you're not personally driving the integration as the CEO, then someone else is, and it might not be in the direction you had envisioned.

Thus, keep in mind who you would trust to lead an acquisition, should it happen. Write a draft plan. Identify areas of weakness where you need help to shut down blind spots.

Part 2
Communication Experiences

Chapter 8

Clarity Not Cleverness

The Cyclone arrived with high energy and unlimited ideas. She led massive B2C teams previously, but now she faced a 100% B2B world and it was a uniquely different game with higher stakes and zero room for missteps. She was smart, ambitious, and determined to make a splash. She wanted it her way, which was "with cleverness."

In every meeting, she bounced from vision to tactics to product roadmap to funding partners in a single meeting. Her ideas came in like a storm, fast and unfiltered. Her mind moved at lighting speed, but her communication style left the senior leadership team (SLT) confused and unclear, leaving more questions than answers. I had a front row seat and was able to observe behind the scenes actions and behaviors.

She spent a few weeks traveling to regional offices, visiting customers, and deciding on who she could trust as her inner circle.

Upon her return to the office, she decided on the names of our initial programs under her guidance. She introduced new terms, new references to channel partners, and new processes. In this chapter, we will focus on one critical lesson: clarity over cleverness.

Some CEOs obsess over cleverness. Clever taglines. Clever emails. Clever slogans. Clever product names. But cleverness doesn't build trust. Clarity does. Coupled with clear expectations, these create a secret to a CEO's (and all leaders') success.

This chapter isn't about bad intentions. It's about the gap between what a CEO says and what their team hears. It's about clarity.

The Mistake

The Cyclone mistook cleverness and energy for clear leadership communication. She believed her big ideas and clever new phrases and terms would energize the company and build momentum.

But quickly, the SLT struggled with her ideas. We didn't know which message to follow, which priorities to chase, or what her expectations were of us. They heard the passion but not the direction. And the result? Chaotic internal discussions about these new programs that used new acronyms and terms. The two big ones were VBO (Value-Based Offers), and SPR/VARSI (Super Value-Added Resellers/ Systems Integrators) Huh? Here is what the team heard:

VBO = lower margins

SPR/VARSI = unclear and impossible to serve

Outcome: frustration and inaction

Her all-hands meetings were master classes in high energy and information charts but left employees walking away with more questions than answers. Her slide decks were filled with wild information and slogans but lacked substance. They were meaningless without context. Our corporate office had a factory floor where we all gathered, but in remote regional offices people gathered around their conference rooms for streamed video.

Setting the Stage

The Cyclone quickly hired people from her previous company because they understood her.

Short-term execution suffered because no one knew what the North Star was. Every week, something new was "top priority." The two business units were rumored to be restructured, so hallway discussions dominated the days. She kept talking program names, terms, and phrases which had no bones yet.

She was so clever. She thought people would be more curious and ask questions about the clever program names, but it backfired. The cleverness became a distraction. One employee bluntly said, "I just wish she'd tell us what she really wants, and then we do it." Clarity was missing.

The Cyclone was successful in her mission to hire her old cronies and create a new level of management. At senior leadership team meetings, one by one she threw each senior leader under the bus in front of their peers per week.

The Decision Process

When the Cyclone came in from her previous general manager role, she had a plan. It is a common occurrence for first-time CEOs who were COOs or GMs to make smoother transitions. COOs and GMs have a solid foundation and understand business functions, financials, and how to drive alignment across them.

The Cyclone decided she would be professional and get to know everyone from day one. Then she would be brutally authoritarian after 30 days and show she was the boss. However, her communication style was more disruptive due to her purposeful ambiguity and lack of clarity.

The Cyclone brought a long-time decision-making process from a very large multibillion dollar multinational corporation to a smaller environment with far less information available to make numbers-based decisions. Previously, she could simply ask one of many "analysts" on her team to get specific data, and it would appear. Our smaller company did not have "analysts," nor did we have the IT systems or people in place to get that data. She chose to hire her old team to help herself get out of the situation she now owned.

This lack of information and resources required the steps she took as follows, which was easy to see in hindsight:

- Confuse the existing team with new terms and ambiguity.

- Embarrass each SLT member in staff meetings weekly to break down people.

- In 1:1 meetings, she would tell each senior team member what they didn't do well, and she would say nothing about what they did well.

- Bring in her friends to interview and never tell the SLT what position they were interviewing for.

- Collect our interview reports (she collected one-page interview feedback from all interviewers).

- Hired her friends into newly created senior level positions.

- Restructured the company; note that there were no layoffs which was a surprise to all employees.

- But the lack of clarity remained, and the terms VBO and SPR/VARSI remained.

The Results

The results of the Cyclone's transition and approach into the company serve as a wake-up call to newly hired CEOs. Every CEO transition is different. Why you were hired and the company's situation shapes the playbook. The board of directors made the decision to change, and now you own the role.

There are books written on the first 90 or 100 days, and they provide sound advice. It may or may not apply to you, just like the Cyclone's story may not apply. But here is what happened, starting with the terms and acronyms:

- VBO = Value Based Offer. The problem was, the Cyclone wanted to bundle several low-margin items together and offer a discount as "value," but the results were lower overall margins. Most leaders took months to understand the concept because they knew the margin situation.

- SPR/VARSI = Super-Sized Value-Added Resellers and System Integrators are the suppliers to many large enterprise and government accounts. They offer packages of "best-of-breed" solutions, meaning they were not interested in one supplier, such as our company, that had pieces of the solution but not best of breed in every networking category. There were insufficient margin points to offer discount levels these super-sized solutions providers were looking for.

- The newly hired senior executives were scheduled to present the "new plan" at the national sales meeting in Las Vegas, but no one understood the Cyclone's presentation with new terms, and lack of clarity but lots of clever acronyms. The Cyclone ended up doing the presentation in front of a thousand people with no preparation. It did not work well.

- Five weeks after this Las Vegas experience, the Cyclone was terminated along with all her new hires. A corporate executive from the parent company took over in the interim to "fix" everything.

- The case was not closed, as the company was not out of the woods due to lack of clarity. It can only be described as pure chaos.

How to Avoid This Mistake

If you're a newly hired CEO, especially from a larger organization into a smaller, fast-paced environment, drop the cleverness and lead with clarity:

- Speak clearly.

- Drop the clever acronyms.

- Define your terms.

- State the why.

- Clarify ownership.

- Gain alignment.

Start every meeting and message with: "Here's what we're doing. Here's why. Here's how." That's it. Ask questions. Ask for the team to play back what they heard. Repeat until clarity is achieved. Simple wins.

As CEO, here is a weekly exercise for you. It is a good ritual to help you become self-aware:

- Are we all focused on the same top three priorities of the week?

- Did the SLT understand everything discussed in our meeting and agree?

- Did you ask the SLT to playback what they heard in the meeting?

Customize for your philosophy and approach, but a personal checklist following every SLT meeting/staff meeting will help you stay fully aware of what you are communicating and if it is clear or not. These days, use an AI-based note taker to record and summarize the meeting. Share the results and ask for agreement. Resolve any open items immediately.

Recovery and Moving Forward

Since you have become the new CEO, you have inherited whatever situation existed with the people in place. You likely already have your own playbook and system to adapt to your new and exciting role. After the Cyclone left, the interim CEO followed this playbook, which you can use as a new CEO transitioning into an existing company:

- **Reset.** Acknowledge the situation and assemble the team of leaders to restart.

- **Simplify all messaging.** Eliminate confusing terms, regardless of whether they were clever or not. Rename initiatives. Gain team confidence by working together.

- **Host a clarity summit.** Hold offsite/neutral site meeting to re-align priorities, initiatives, identify the hottest and highest priority items, and reset expectations.

- **Rebuild trust.** Clarity isn't just about words. It includes consistency. The interim CEO showed the team he would lead with clear expectations, clear communications, and leaving no questions unanswered.

Clarity rebuilds confidence and clear expectations drive success.

Conclusion

Clever ideas and words can stop the scroll. There is a time for use of cleverness, maybe for advertisements! For CEOs and leaders, clarity earns trust, and leadership is based on trust, integrity, clear expectations, and clear communications.

When CEOs trade clarity for cleverness, people get lost. Priorities blur. Execution stalls. You don't win by sounding clever. You win by being clear.

As a CEO, every word you speak becomes important. Every employee, leader or not, hangs onto every word you say. If it's not clear, you lose respect and trust from the people. Choose clarity. Always.

Secret #8: Clarity is your superpower. Confusion kills culture. Keep it simple. Set clear expectations early. Confirm understanding consistently.

Chapter 9

Micromanagement and Delegation

Micromanagement does not look like a blind spot, until it becomes a costly one.

Lexi, a first-time founder and CEO of an IT services firm, prided himself on running a flat organization. No middle managers. Just him and the team.

It worked for a while.

Lexi had led a large IT team inside a very large enterprise company prior to his startup, so the challenge of owning everything in a company was new and, at times, overwhelming. He applied previous management techniques he learned from a book (this is not unusual) to manage his "flat" organizational structure. His philosophy was to operate his company as flatly as possible, as it eliminated a level of management or two that the CEO covered.

Techniques Lexi learned in his previous company led to his biggest mistakes which fell into the micromanagement category. Micromanagement has been written about at length in books, articles, and educational courses. But, for our story, consider why CEOs and leaders become micromanagers: they fear failure, they have imposter syndrome, they have insecurities about their own skill sets, and possibly they lack trust of their team members. They want to maintain control.

Do you see yourself here? Read on to learn about Lexi's journey.

The Mistake

Lexi held two mandatory stand-up meetings per day addressing planning the day (early morning), followed by accountability, what each team member had accomplished at the close of business (late afternoon).

Lexi thought this was structure. His team called it surveillance and oversight.

This is old-school micromanagement and typically despised by most, if not all, team members. Consider how this impacts corporate culture and morale. As a reminder, people leave jobs because of their manager, their situation, their lack of job satisfaction, and other reasons, with micromanagement being near the top of the list as one of those other reasons.

Setting the Stage

Short of revenue targets and deadlines missed, Lexi felt he had to tighten everyone's leash! He became intensely involved in every detail of every project regardless of how small, which was not well received by his team.

Through advisory work with one of Lexi's senior team members, the full scope of this micromanagement became crystal clear. The recordings of these team meetings revealed the detailed inquisition that every individual faced twice daily in front of their peers.

Imagine how these team members felt.

The Decision Process

As mentioned previously, Lexi did have a go-to process and pre-meeting daily form that every individual had to email to him by 8:30 am daily for the day's planned tasks. As it turned out, his form included career goals, what three things you were doing every day/week/month to achieve your goals, and some additional but not necessarily important outside-of-work activities you might be participating in. Lexi would then believe he had full control of you, because he learned what was driving your daily life.

It's a good idea to meet 1:1 with your team members on a regular basis such as weekly, monthly, or quarterly but not twice daily. It's also a good idea to know about their goals, and to learn how you can help them remove roadblocks and obstacles.

Part 4 of this book will discuss decision-making frameworks and processes. Lexi's micromanagement falls into the "analysis paralysis" type of leadership decision-making, where the CEO collects far too much data which is not necessary to lead with and prevents the concept of building trust.

The Results

You can probably figure out that, at this point, people resigned or revolted regarding the twice daily stand-up meetings, as it was overkill micromanagement. People wrote wild stories on the form for the Lexi to read, and seeing if he would say anything about them. Was he really reading these and, if so, how was he using the information?

Having senior team members resign can impact projects, revenues, morale, and severely break the company culture. This occurred, and it took many months to adjust Lexi's expectations and CEO behavior. Projects were missed with the daily meetings as attitudes soured, and the process backfired.

Also consider how the employees that remain feel having to cover for their departed colleagues and friends.

How to Avoid This Mistake

Experience managing both small and large groups of employees shows that, twice daily check-ins are only required for extremely high profile, short-term customer project deliverables, which may have financial penalties for missing milestones. I have experienced and led these meetings at times. These are special circumstances the team understands. But Lexi's approach was normal operating mode for him.

Lexi could have avoided all the micromanagement issues if he used a proven leadership process, which includes SMART Goals, Scorecards, KPIs, and/or OKRs reporting on a weekly basis with a monthly summary, if necessary. In *The Rookie CEO* book, I write about the Opportunist's use of monthly scorecards for all managers, directors, and vice presidents that are openly shared and combined with a published culture code to fully fuel team members helping and supporting one another to achieve goals.

Thirty-five-plus years of senior leadership experience shows that the top three to five priorities, status of each, and obstacles or blockers preventing progress from the past week with plans for the following week are effective reporting methods. At one company, adding a "what keeps you up at night" section led to immediate meetings with that team leader to resolve any blockers. Each company is different, so you need to find the right mix for both leadership and team members to be effective, satisfied, and productive.

Lexi did not use any of these techniques.

As CEO, consider alternatives to Lexi's approach.

Recovery and Moving Forward

Although my client left the company to escape the micro-management madness, we were able to track everything that happened due to people who remained with Lexi. He eventually moved to one daily stand-up meeting, but the team members never really recovered from the micromanagement bug of the CEO.

The only reason many people stayed at the company was the evolution of AI projects that interested the technical team members.

The company is still in existence as of this writing and is slowly growing again, but did he learn anything? Lexi stayed in control.

Conclusion

Micromanagement is one of the most damaging leadership habits a CEO can develop. Lexi's reliance on twice-daily stand-up meetings, invasive personal tracking, and rigid oversight broke employee trust, drove away talented employees, and damaged both morale and productivity. His company's struggles with missed deadlines, stalled projects, and resignations were entirely predictable.

The lesson here is simple but critical: leaders must empower, not control. A CEO should create an environment where talented employees can perform at their best, not one where they feel suffocated by constant oversight. Delegation, trust, structure and accountability measures such as SMART goals, KPIs, OKRs, and reporting create high-functioning teams that support each other.

Lexi did not realize that control is not the same as leadership. His blind spot was trust.

For CEOs reading this, let Lexi's story be a lesson for you: If you treat senior employees like junior interns, they will leave. If you don't trust your people, they won't trust you.

Success in leadership comes from hiring great people, setting clear goals, giving them the autonomy to execute, and holding them accountable for results and outcomes, not for every minute of their day. The trend towards working remote has increased CEO anxiety in executing and accomplishing these processes which can be easily modified to include your remote workers.

If you find yourself in a micromanagement cycle, stop and take a step back. Ask yourself: Am I giving my team the space to do their best work? If not, adjust, before they walk away. If you create a culture of micromanagement, you won't build a company that lasts.

Here are red flags for CEO's micromanagement:

- Asking for daily updates.

- Rewrite team member's work frequently.

- You get anxious if you can't "see" activity.

- Your 1:1 status meeting focuses on hindsight, not how they are doing and how can you help them advance their work by removing obstacles.

- Your team hesitates to make decisions without your signoff.

Secret #9: Hire great people and set clear expectations and goals. Trust them to deliver. Micromanagement is a culture killer. Replace it with autonomy, support, curiosity, and accountability.

Chapter 10

Employee Feedback

Like the warnings on your side mirror "objects that may be closer than they appear" employee feedback often signals what's coming.

Consider Boeing's 737 MAX disaster history, where internal engineers raised red flag warnings that leadership ignored, CEOs who dismiss internal feedback do so at their peril. Blind spots can be seen by others but not necessarily you. You need to listen.

Employee and leadership team feedback loops seem to be ignored by many CEOs, especially first-time CEOs. Why this is true boggles my mind. One of the easiest things a CEO can do is to build into the culture a methodology to capture feedback. My long-time argument is that people around you can see your blind spots; you can't see them.

You may know that you can't see around the corner, but someone else can see that spot that is blind to you. I debate this concept with a few CEOs. It's an awareness blind spot to ignore blind spots!

The Mistake

Let's explore two CEO mistakes that could have easily been prevented but caused tremendous loss of employee trust, respect, and commitment to their success.

1. The Sales Schemer: the Opportunist had a sales manager who was showing serious irregularities in his conduct and monthly reports. Others in the company were able to point out inconsistent sales activities, and shared recorded evidence of practices (all company calls not on cell phones were recorded) that did not align with company standards.

    They included booking new deals each month that were canceled within 30 days. Commissions were paid and quota relief to the President's Club was given to both the sales leader and his channel, which in turn skewed both sales and churn rates. One other major flaw was changing "seller of record" to existing accounts that took commission payments away from the true seller and gave credit to himself.

2. The Lone Wolf Promise: another CEO, Robert, took on an opportunity with a major customer that was undoable. But, at an all-hands meeting, he asked

everyone at the startup to work more hours, work smarter, and make the unrealistic deliverable dates.

He could have talked with his leadership team to gain buy-in or get ideas, but he just committed to the customer and to the private investors and told everyone what needed to happen while he was on the road. Many employees questioned him at the all-hands meeting, and one asked about employee mental health. On that day, he wrote off that person who asked that question and she never recovered.

Setting the Stage

The sales leader befriended the Opportunist, charmed his wife, and worked the system. He knew the comp plans, the commission games, and the loopholes. He used every one of them.

Robert had done a terrific founder-led sales job with one of the top companies in the world with the largest data centers to gain a trial of our products. But to get tested and deployed, there was a tight schedule, and the hot new products were not ready to be deployed yet. Tested yes, but deployed in production into one of the world's largest highest visible networks? No way.

But as a high energy, passionate "want to win" founder CEO, he committed to deliver and then came back to his all-hands meeting to "tell" everyone what was required.

There was no plan to gain buy-in to lead the teams into this challenge. The engineers, quality assurance, and product teams did have major issues and felt left out of the discussions.

The Decision Process

Each CEO has their own decision process. Part 4 of this book is all about the decision process most CEOs and leaders have which is often an "automatic" style of decision that each has developed over their entire life.

This style is part of PPLC, introduced in *The Rookie CEO* and based on the CEO's personal leadership approach shaped by background, philosophy, and lived experiences (P=Path to Ceo, P=Philosophy, L=Leadership Style, and C=Culture).

Robert had a huge multimillion dollar opportunity early in the company's life, and all he had to do was "make it happen" among his hand selected team and friends. He did not expect as much pushback as he got and certainly did not expect to lose the opportunity. He had built a top-level relationship with this customer and truly felt he was doing what was right. It was hard to fault Robert, except in his team communications style.

The Results

The sales leader's boss was terminated and replaced. A new vice president of sales was recruited. The sales leader who was pulling the wool over the Opportunist's eyes was eventually terminated.

Robert's mistake did not just miss a launch. It fractured his team's belief in him. That was harder to fix than a late project. That customer purchased a few million dollars' worth of products, but the big data center expansion was missed. And the damage was done inside to the culture. It's debatable if Robert ever recovered from this, and one could debate either side.

Everyone learned a lot, all were able to get back to collaborate more on newer opportunities. Since then, most of the people from that early team are long gone from the company.

How to Avoid This Mistake

There are simple strategies to avoid these types of mistakes. For the sales mistakes, have a solid sales process, sales management process, revenue and commission recognition process, and if customers churn, stop paying out commission for those subscriptions that canceled. Follow the process. Hold sales leadership at all levels accountable, and do not give President's Club (or whatever you call your top sales achievement award) credit until after a set probationary period to prove the sale is real and not a "channel stuffing" exercise.

Today, the position overseeing these are called "Revenue Operations" or Revops. Additionally, new AI tools provide all the data needed to create a real-time dashboard of all relevant data.

For the aggressive commitment to deliver product when it's not ready, regardless of the customer profile, the leadership team must collaborate on what is achievable and how. Sometimes, paying a premium for expedited test and certifications might get you there, but the team executing the job must buy in and be given every tool and dollar necessary. Otherwise, you walk away and stay on task for your future. This was a unilateral CEO decision.

Recovery and Moving Forward

The Opportunist recovered well. The new Sales VP restructured sales, the channel records were cleaned up and discrepancies resolved. The company was acquired with a good earn out. The key was to take out the resource that was breaking the rules and replace them with trusted leaders who followed the sales process and company rules.

Robert's recovery has not been as smooth as the Opportunist's recovery. He worked hard to include the team more in anything requiring aggressive dates and commitments. It has improved as well as new people were added without the history of this mistake.

Conclusion

Ignoring employee feedback is one of the most preventable mistakes a CEO can make. There are times when the CEO likes the employee who appears to be loyal, but he is twisting a knife into your back with a smile. This person's boss was providing the feedback and proof! But the Opportunist chose to ignore it.

The Opportunist was able to learn and grow from this experience when he brought in the new sales leader. It was one of those experiences that will likely never happen again.

Robert, on the other hand, made a different kind of error, committing the company to an impossible promise without first aligning his leadership team. His passion and confidence, though admirable, led to several unhappy employees.

What makes Robert's situation difficult is that most startups must commit to unreasonable delivery of their products or services to win the deal. It can also happen to an established company with a new product or a new release in a highly competitive or contentious deal. In some cases, it could be millions of dollars in revenues.

It is a good practice for CEOs to create and implement a process with their leadership team on how to evaluate and tackle these types of commitments to win the deal. But it is a "must" to involve the team to get buy-in and agreement.

In the end, listening is not just a leadership tactic, it is a strategy.

Secret #10: Your senior leadership team are your partners and first line of collaboration; leverage and trust them. Get commitment and buy-in from your team to achieve the big life-changing wins. Loyalty is earned through listening. Blind spots can be addressed and eliminated through feedback flows.

Chapter 11

Google Ads (PPC), Agencies, and Performance Marketing

Lubdo didn't just waste $350,000. He nearly lost his company chasing "the easy button" of Google Ads.

For first-time CEOs and founders, especially technically skilled ones, Pay-Per-Click (PPC) feels like magic. Until it becomes a money pit and drains cash.

He created a good product, had won customers, and offered a free and paid version. The free download is commonly called Product Led Growth (PLG) as a go-to-market model. With his lack of sales and marketing background, and his "basic training" from Y Combinator (YC), he felt Google Ads (PPC) were the "easy button" to potential customers.

As an engineer, he loved the Google Ads Console and the challenge to "win" customers.

Startup accelerators often teach "performance marketing" as a fast measurable method to generate leads to gain new customers. Performance marketing is Google Ads, which are pay-per-click and, to be effective, it takes serious experience and in-depth understanding. Google Ads have a place, but spending *all* your marketing dollars on them is a huge flaw in a marketing strategy. Knowing the exact target customer (ICP, or ideal customer profile), and the keywords they would be searching for exactly are key elements of Google Ads. Get them wrong, and it's burning cash.

Lubdo hired two agencies. One for SEO (search engine optimization) and one as a substitute for a marketing head. He committed $61,000 per month, pre-paid for six and three months respectively. There was no one who knew how to manage these agencies. There was no progress, just wasted cash.

Lubdo had a handful of trusted advisors from his past and from his investors, who provided suggestions of hiring a marketing head which he did, to resolve the problems and sort out the agency and Google Ad expensive headaches.

The Mistakes

There are two mistakes here:

- Mistake #1: Agency Overload:

    a. A full-service firm that he thought would replace a marketing head

    b. An SEO agency

    Agencies can work but require an inside champion to manage and drive priorities, track spending, and manage projects.

- Mistake #2: Google Ads Obsession

    Lubdo chose to ignore all suggestions from his advisors to not use Google Ads, where he was spending another $35K/month. They all told him to use other lower cost but effective marketing tools such as content marketing, blog posts, and social media.

Setting the Stage

Lubdo was not just running Google Ads, he was feeding his ego.

Lubdo believed he knew better than anyone and loved the challenge of Google Ads and tracking clicks. He felt it was working. He was emotionally connected to each click, because his mind told him it was the "easy button" to customers.

He finally hired a full-time contractor as the marketing head as requested by his lead investor.

She repeatedly told him Google Ads were not converting. He ignored her feedback which is a serious mistake by a CEO. Direct feedback can eliminate blind spots, but ignoring her feedback, he ignored his blind spot, which drained most of his venture investment.

A couple of other pieces of data that he was misinformed about included:

- Thinking that Google impressions could be used for funding. His lead investor laughed at this idea. But this vanity metric concept of impressions means eyeballs, not revenue or conversions!

- He also was convinced that, if he could get onto page one of the Google for key search terms, he would become a billion-dollar company. His marketer got the company onto page one of Google, but it did not move the revenue needle.

The Decision Process

For Lubdo, his decision was ego-based "I know better than everyone else," and he chose not to listen to his new experienced senior marketer or his investors, totally ignoring feedback from experts.

Imagine a Customer Relations Management (CRM) tool where every click was labeled as a "deal". This is what Lubdo built.

It took hours of manual work to reverse engineer conversions from Google Ads, which in this case exposed they were not converting.

To be fair, many first-time CEOs make similar mistakes. It might be a different marketing tactic, but the founder or first-time CEO lock onto one thing, don't test it to validate that it works, and they waste time and spend valuable cash on it. They also mix up vanity metrics with measurable revenue generating metrics and ROI, or return on the investment.

The Results

"One small customer. Ten months. Thirty-Five Grand per month." Google Ads.

New marketing programs introduced by the marketing head started to double revenues as well as inspire existing customers to upgrade and increase ACV (Annual Contract Value). These programs included regularly scheduled events that were twenty to thirty minutes in length, featuring Lubdo demonstrating new features and how to solve problems with the software tool. These events were open to prospects and existing customers, and the resulting videos went into a resource library on the website and on YouTube. These were the best performing lead generation programs.

Despite this success, the damage was done as 90% of the venture funding was spent. Most of the company was laid off, including one cofounder, and the few remaining employees (mostly sales) took an 80% cut in salary.

How to Avoid This Mistake

There are some lessons for ALL CEOs here.

- Listen to your advisors and your senior marketer (senior leadership team).

- Track all spend in detail and know where every dollar goes.

- Don't fall in love with something that is "fun" for you, and it is not even your job in the company (you are CEO, running ads should not your role).

- Get a coach that can help you uncover your blind spots and address them. These mistakes were both due to blind spots that could have been avoided completely.

See the conclusion that follows for a suggested playbook!

Recovery and Moving Forward

The company did not go under. He cut Google Ad expenditures. He focused on technical SEO and content. It is more of "the long game" but, done properly, starts to generate organic leads without ad spend.

Content that was created during the marketer's tenure still exists and generates leads consistently with sales conversions. The resource library became an evergreen lead generator.

Budget constraints are tight from his investors as Lubdo receives amounts of funding to match operating needs and has maintained small but steady revenue growth with his sales resources.

The ACV has increased which helps the company potentially scale.

Lubdo still has a lot to learn, but he listens more to his investors, advisors, and management team.

Conclusion

The best way that you, as the CEO with founder-led marketing responsibilities, can avoid Lubdo's mistakes might be to consider this playbook to power your marketing, generate sales, and avoid money pits:

- Start building your CEO brand on LinkedIn or your chosen social channel; you can hire a coach to help for a reasonable amount of budget. There are excellent advisors, mentors, and coaches out there.

- Find product-market-fit before spending on innovative marketing programs and/or Google Ads.

- Hire a marketing leader to own the strategy and manage any outside resources.

- Test programs and ads with small buckets of cash before larger spend to prove out what works, if performance marketing is your goal.

- Explore strategies with the marketing lead such as inbound, outbound, partnerships, and events.

- Create a newsletter as you build a database of prospects through lead magnets and programs from your marketer. This is a great tool to share events and your resource library.

- Listen to feedback from your team, advisors, and investors as experience has its merits especially with first-time CEOs.

- And, as always, recommended: listen, learn, and ask questions!

Bonus: Checklist for your marketing budget (adapt to your business)

- Track real conversion rates, not just clicks and impressions.

- Have clear ownership over ALL external spending.

- Ensure your ICP (ideal customer profile) is clear, and you understand their buying triggers.

- Have a new tactic to try? Test it for less than $5K before scaling into higher-priced programs.

- Is your activity tied to actual revenue growth, or is it just visibility?

Secret #11: Paid ads are not the "easy button." Create your playbook, using this chapter's example modified for your company. Marketing is a full suite of brand building, demand generation, and messaging with your ideal prospects; hire your internal champion, test small, and scale with real insights, not impressions.

Part 3
People

Chapter 12

Don't Worry, There Are Twenty-Six Hours in a Day!

Every CEO says they'll hire help when they're too busy.

Bob didn't, he waited too long. It cost him speed, sanity, and scale.

Bob is the President and CEO of a Southern California-based managed service provider (MSP). He learned firsthand the impact of not fully grasping the responsibilities of a CEO and the timing for hiring critical resources.

Bob's story is about delaying decisions that he knew he should have addressed. Bob's experience is a wake-up call to trust their instincts and act decisively when the need arises.

The Mistake

In the early stages, Bob didn't just wait. He knew what he needed but talked himself out of doing it for years. Bob's mistake was waiting too long to "let go" and bring in two essential hires: an operations manager and a dedicated salesperson.

He pushed forward, believing he could continue handling it all. However, he soon found out that doing too much, especially tasks he didn't enjoy, was not sustainable.

The company's business model initially centered on product sales with add-on maintenance services. Over time, Bob successfully transitioned to a managed services model, creating a steady stream of recurring revenue. Reflecting, Bob admits that had he hired those key resources sooner, the company would have scaled faster. He makes no excuses; he learned a valuable lesson about the CEO's role in scaling and sustainability.

Setting the Stage

Bob's company was in a phase of rapid growth. He was doing it all and doing it well, staying within his self-imposed fifty-hour limit. But as the business grew, he reached a breaking point. The workload began to exceed the 50-hour measure, setting the stage for his eventual mistake. Every new hour he carved out got filled with more work.

Bob was handling support, ops, client issues, vendor relationships, and sales, all while trying to scale. Every day stretched longer. Customers loved him, but his calendar was overbooked.

It took nearly a decade for Bob to fully understand how it impacted the company's growth. At the time, he was so focused on maintaining profit margins and EBITDA that he overlooked the necessity of bringing in new talent, fearing it would lower the bottom line.

The Decision Process

Bob's thought process was influenced by his perspective of profit and Earnings Before Interest, Taxes, Depreciation, and Amortization (EBITDA). He knew he didn't enjoy certain operational and sales tasks, but he found comfort in the company's financial performance. His customer-centric approach, symbolized by giving clients his personal cell number for 24/7 support, was a standout feature in the crowded Southern California MSP market. His mission was clear: take the pain away from the customer and to be indispensable to everyone.

Bob prided himself on his 24/7 support policy, but he was struggling silently in his mind.

Bob's approach came at a cost that he did not fully understand at the time. He delayed hiring his key resources, because he was convinced that cutting into his profits wasn't worth it. He loved the control and the success. But he ignored the reality that no one person can do it all effectively as the business scales.

The Results

Once Bob finally hired his key resources, everything changed for the better. Yes, EBITDA took a hit, but it settled into a more realistic figure. The payoff? Bob's life improved dramatically, and the company began to thrive. He realized that hiring smarter people than himself for key positions and doing so earlier would have accelerated the company's growth. The ultimate lesson: focus on what you do best and love to do, and hire for everything else!

This shift positioned the company for long-term success, and eventually, it was acquired. Bob remains the President and CEO, now leading a team filled with empowered leaders in essential roles.

How to Avoid This Mistake

Bob's story emphasizes a simple truth: act with speed and purpose! If your calendar is full of work you don't like to do, it's not hustle. It's self-sabotage. Bob was guilty of this.

Bill Miller

Recovery and Moving Forward

The recovery process wasn't instant; it was a decade-long journey. Bob gradually learned to empower his hires, although he admits that even now, it can take him over a year to fully trust and delegate responsibilities. His advice to fellow CEOs is to speed up this process. The sooner you trust your team, the sooner you can capitalize on their expertise and propel the company forward.

Bob also highlights the importance of being open to new ideas brought by your key hires. As a CEO, understanding what "good" looks like and being self-aware enough to recognize your own gaps will set the foundation for long-term success.

Ask Yourself:

- Are you the bottleneck in operations or sales?

- What task drains you that someone else could own?

- What hire have you been putting off for three or more months?

- Are your EBITDA targets killing your team's capacity?

- Would your company run better if you stepped back from execution?

89

- If you stepped away for a week's vacation, would sales keep going? Would clients be supported? Would anything break?

If yes, delegate more. If no, hire now!

Conclusion

Bob's experience resonates with CEOs at every stage of their journey. Delaying critical decisions, such as hiring key personnel, can cost your company valuable time, revenue, and credibility in the market.

Let your team do their jobs while you focus on leading the company toward its goals. Leadership isn't just about making popular decisions. It's also about making the right ones, even when they're tough.

Bob wants to leave all CEOs with this John Wooden quote: "Whatever you do in life, surround yourself with smart people who'll argue with you."

Secret #12: Don't delay when it's time to hire. Move fast, empower fully, and get out of the way. Waiting too long to bring in the right person will cost you time, traction, and trust. Your gut already knows what the role needs. Do it! Hire. Delegate. And let them run. Smart CEOs don't just build teams; they also trust them to deliver.

Chapter 13

Build Your A-Team: Hiring Secrets Every CEO Needs to Know

Every CEO has a hiring regret. A cofounder who was a mismatch. A VP who did not execute. The mistake? Rushing the hire. The fix? Build a system.

Ask any CEO what haunts them years later, and they most likely will not say it was a missed forecast or a bad quarter. They will tell you, "I hired the wrong person," or worse, "I hired the wrong cofounder."

The Mistake

The Opportunist was introduced in *The Rookie CEO, You Can't Make This Stuff Up!* His company had excellent products and services; however, they were experiencing stagnation issues. They had a head of customer support who had an attitude problem. The Opportunist had hired someone who was not vetted properly which drove customer satisfaction ratings down and led to increasing churn rates. It was easy to spot. By listening to customer call recordings. This could have been prevented. The Opportunist let it go on far too long. He asked for help. He had hired this leader "on the spot" because of his likeability and the belief that he could manage and control this person.

Many CEOs have structured interview processes they have built over the years from day one, and pre-day one for founder selection. Leaders learn on their way to CEO about interviewing and finding their ideal candidates, but the fact that some interviewees who have flawless educational backgrounds, are well spoken, and are extremely bright does not always translate to success.

Do not be fooled by what "looks good on paper" or even "sounds too smooth" (likeable) to be true.

Setting the Stage

Hiring and retaining the "right" leadership team is a key to CEO success. Be intentional in hiring the right team. Be intentional about onboarding new leaders. Be intentional in terminating improper fits. Your definition of improper fits is critical, because you want leaders who challenge you, brainstorm with you, and align with you once agreement is achieved. Do not hire a "yes" person. They will disrupt your success.

The Decision Process

The decision process on vetting your new hire direct reports will become one of your career-long success factors. Learning and applying best practices to accompany your personal style, the involvement of your team, and matching your company's core values and culture with the candidates are crucial success factors.

This hiring process can be an industry accepted standard or one you have created and modified from your previous experiences. For example, working with a human resources consultant and the Opportunist who wanted to improve his hiring of A-players for his senior leadership team, the HR consultant shared her combination of two methods, "Topgrading" developed by Brad Smart in the 1990s but evolved over the years and the "Who Method" developed by Geoff Smart (Brad Smart's son) and Randy Street which you can find in the book, *Who*.

For clarity, the Topgrading method focuses on in-depth chronological interviews and the Who method emphasizes scorecards, structured and focused interviews, and reference calls as its core.

Each process can be used on its own, but the Opportunist combined these for all hires, not just A-player executives. Every new hire went through a comprehensive multiple rounds of interviews and were graded on their core competencies, scored against the company's core competencies and core values, and in-depth behavioral interviews. This works for startups as well as businesses of other sizes. The time invested in hiring paid off.

The Results

A selected quarterback collected data, worked with the Opportunist by creating a spreadsheet score tracker from each interviewer. Only the quarterback knew the scores. When all rounds were completed, all interviewers met in one meeting, discussed scores and tradeoffs, and any candidate who did not meet their A-player criteria was eliminated. The final two candidates were deeply reference-checked prior to any offer.

The leaders of all groups except one were replaced and upgraded to prepare the company for growth and acquisition. The results were excellent. To be honest, it takes a village, an old cliché that applies here, but it takes a serious effort to hire the right team and position the company for growth and potential exit.

How to Avoid Making a Mistake

Mis-hires can cost the company ten to fifteen times (varies by source but is in this range) the executive salary. That's too much money to not take hiring seriously. Talent is easy to find. A-player talent that fits all levels of core competencies and culture is challenging and not easy to find and hire.

Today, with new tools and AI (artificial intelligence), it becomes easy to overlook the challenges of hiring your ideal A-player executives. Do not take the easy path. Find your ideal method that balances in-depth capabilities and speed of the process.

When your new hire starts, create an onboarding plan, execute this plan rapidly, and ensure there is a thirty-six-ty-ninety (30-60-90) day plan that resulted from the interview process. A scorecard for this hire provides clarity on deliverables and outcomes.

If you do not see success within each thirty-day window (which can be a measured sprint), take rapid action to replace the hire. You may find out during this period the candidate lied on their resume (again, various sources estimate that fifty to 75% of candidates lie) and they are unable to execute as the A-player you thought you'd hired.

Recovery and Moving Forward

If you find that you make a mistake once your new hire starts, and you have measured results that are not achieving desired results, you have two choices. Option one is to terminate immediately. Option two is to create an improvement plan with criteria for short-term success. The Opportunist was a "fire fast" CEO. Thus, he chose option one in each case.

If you choose option one, go back to your process. Refine it for where you missed with this hire, and do not make the same mistake again.

Conclusion

All CEOs I have ever worked for, with, or interviewed have clearly stated their success is driven by their senior leadership team.

The secret is implementing a hiring process that integrates core competencies of the individual and the company. Do the work and follow your process to bring your leadership team together and enhance your hiring success rate.

For first-time CEOs, mastering the art of hiring A-players is not optional, it's your first true leadership multiplier. Here is an **8-step hiring framework** to help guide successful hiring:

Step 1: Install a hiring process that removes guesswork, exposes patterns, and attracts high-caliber talent that scales with you.

Consider applying the Topgrading method or the Who method. The key is to lead from the front.

Step 2: Build a scorecard with specifics and clarity including detailed measurable results and outcomes.

Step 3: Interview with a "focused" approach, with each team member owning a specific range of questions for one to two core competencies. Ideas to split the "focus" include technical capabilities, team player approach, personality, core competencies, likability, and culture fit. Assign the appropriate team member. The CEO most often owns the culture portion of the interview but can ask anything in their interview. Each interviewer fills out an interview score for the quarterback to track and turns it in without talking to other interviewers yet; this will happen at the roundtable.

Step 4: The designated quarterback collects each score immediately after each interview. After all are collected, he/she creates the top-level candidate scorecard. In my experience, these ratings can vary widely in a surprising way.

Step 5: The scoring roundtable is used to discuss the master scores and ideally is projected on the screen for all to see. Each interviewer can present and backup their scores. Open discussions allow score changes up or down depending upon what is discussed. The Opportunist said when the top scored candidate was not acceptable to him, "I'd destroy this guy! He can't deal with me, so he's a hard NO!"

Step 6: Identify the top three candidates and decide who to reference-check. Do not check more than two candidates, but the recommendation is to check only your ideal top candidate. Selection must be a unanimous "yes" to move forward.

Step 7: Reference checks: If you use the Topgrading method, you can ask the candidate to set up calls for you with their former managers/bosses, peers, and direct reports. If they resist any of this, it is a red flag, but you can determine this based on the stories they tell.

Skipping this step can be costly for CEOs. A hidden secret: Do not confuse likeability with leaders who can drive results and desired outcomes. It is difficult to separate chemistry from culture and operational fit based on their core competencies.

Step 8: Reviewing the references. Which person makes the reference calls varies by company and the CEO's philosophy. In my experience, it has been the quarterback, the CEO, or the human resources leader. There is no room for ambiguity here. Mistakes are costly.

CEO Takeaways:

- Hiring mistakes can be the most expensive mistakes and can cost as much as fifteen times the salary.

- Your best hires align with core values and core competencies regardless of skills.

- Once you discover the hiring and onboarding process that works for your company, make it repeatable and the standard process. No shortcuts.

- Create scorecards, leverage structured and focused interviews, and check references.

- Fire fast if the fit is wrong, even after the process is followed. It happens, but you have reduced risk by following your process. Modify the process after a mis-hire.

- You don't need to be perfect, but you do need to be disciplined. Follow your process. Hire slow, fire fast, and repeat what works.

- CEOs who use structured interviews, scorecards, and reference checks outperform their "gut instinct" peers in retention and performance.

Special Bonus: If you would like to receive a *scorecard template*, send an email to bill@billmillertheCEOguy.com with the subject: Scorecard template.

Secret #13: Do not ever hire a candidate on a "gut feeling" on the spot. Vet them properly through the hiring process that integrates and maps core competencies of the individual and the company. Adapt my eight-step framework to your company and make it happen. Your A-team starts here.

Chapter 14

Supercharge Your Employees: Development and Training

CEOs often assume hiring great talent is enough. But if you don't grow your team, they will quit. Or worse, stay and stall progress and growth. Execution breaks down when growth outpaces leadership.

Richard Branson says, "Train people well enough they can leave, treat them well enough so they don't want to!"

In almost every company I have worked with in the past twenty years, the CEO feels there is no time or money to invest in their hires. Are their companies too reactive to scale?

These cause mistakes that can create different levels of draining burnout and unhappy people who choose to leave and can be extremely costly.

The Mistake: Failing to Create a Learning Culture Early On

Many well-known CEOs and founders made these mistakes, and we will discuss them in this chapter. We will also address CEOs and companies from *The Rookie CEO, You Can't Make This Stuff Up!* book as well as other CEOs. Here is a short list of mistakes that CEOs of startups and first-time CEOs make:

- Hiring and believing that smart, experienced, senior hires will "just figure it out."

- Failure to provide coaching, upskilling, or training.

- Senior leaders do not get feedback, guidance, or opportunity to grow.

- Ignoring growth until performance problems arise.

- The CEO's rationalization: we are too busy right now to train or coach.

With the fastest ever emerging technology as I write this book, in the AI (artificial intelligence) and AI tool space, and most parts of the tech stack within every company, training is mandatory for automation, productivity, and growth to scale.

Setting the Stage

In the early stages of startups, the founder CEO is the head salesperson because it's their vision, they know the product or service best, and they are responsible to find all early customers. Therefore, they should hire those who execute and wear multiple hats for their first employees. People who GSD (Get Stuff Done) are critical.

As the company grows, if the CEO does not believe in investing in the people, the requirements outgrow the employees, at all levels, and this is where deliverables start to suffer.

Missed deadlines, features that do not work as advertised and disappointed early customers all drive inconsistency. This does not happen everywhere, but it happens more frequently than one would think.

One CEO I coached told me, "We are moving too fast to stop the momentum and train my team!" On one of our calls six months later, he said, "I think we need to grow our people after all. Can you help me?"

The Decision Process

The CEO must make a commitment to the team: grow the people faster than the company is growing. This becomes a core value decision for the company!

The CEO can talk to investors, advisors, coaches, and peers. There are many peer groups, such as Vistage and YPO (Young President's Organization) that help CEOs address these challenges. Depending on the company type, company stage, and company structure, a learning culture can be implemented alongside day-to-day tasks and functions.

Here are some ideas to consider that CEOs I've coached have implemented:

- Leadership Labs once per month or quarter: founders, leaders, and managers address real team challenges in lunch-and-learns or offsite sessions.

- Coaching Office Hours every other week or month that bring in a group coach for senior leaders who then transfer these learnings to their teams. All sports teams have coaches, from head coaches to specific role/position coaches, and the business should also have coaches.

- Mentorship by creating a "buddy" program coupling individual contributors with senior leaders to challenge them. It develops and grooms the best.

- Internal "Grow Talks" with engineers teaching other engineers, sales and product personnel sharing best practices, and so on. Customize for your company.

CEOs can drive a learning culture where people want to work there, and employees want to stay there. Be the architect of your culture, and lead from the top, setting the example.

The fact is, as CEO, you can be intentional about your culture being a "learning culture," not reactive from day one! Commit to one principle: grow your people faster than your company is growing. Make growth a strategic lever, not an HR function!

The Results

You should experience, within 90-180 days, depending on company stage and size:

- Productivity improvements, for example, reduced issue escalation to leaders and the CEO.

- Employees engagement increases.

- Employees thrive on opportunity and culture.

- You can sleep at night, and finally step back and work *on* the business, not in it.

How to Avoid This Mistake

For first-time and startup CEOs, here's your playbook:

- Coach your leaders. Don't assume they've done this before.

- Start early and small. Even a three-person team can build rituals/habits that scale.

- Create a "learn and teach" culture. Reward those who grow others.

- Use feedback as fuel. Celebrate team wins and create a 360-degree feedback loop.

- Visible Recognition. Spotlight team members who teach others.

The secret to make this successful is create your company playbook on or before day one. A side benefit with this approach is that you reduce blind spots.

Recovery and Moving Forward

If you've already skipped over the entire concept of training and developing your people, which is not unusual, it's not too late.

Start with one:

- **Announce your commitment at an all-hands meeting.** Tell your team you're investing in their growth from here on out.

- **Pick one internal program to pilot;** consider either the Leadership Lab idea or a Mentorship Program.

- **Ask your leaders where they feel stuck.** Begin to shape your training and coaching focus. It's recommended to ask this question in private 1:1 meetings.

- **Make your programs visible.** Celebrate all wins.

Note: You're not "too small" for training. Do not delay it any longer.

Bonus Section #1: Lessons from the Trenches: CEOs Who Got it Wrong First

- Early on, in Airbnb's growth, Brian Chesky, co-founder and CEO, said they did not invest enough in leadership development (source: Masters of Scale Podcast). He brought in executive coaches, created scorecards, and personally invested his time in helping his leaders.

- Stewart Butterfield, cofounder and CEO of Slack, said they underestimated the importance of developing leaders and managers which slowed the company early on (source: First Round Review).

- Ben Horowitz, cofounder and former CEO of Opsware, explained in his book, *The Hard Thing About Hard Things*, how lack of leadership development nearly broke the company before it scaled. He said, "I didn't realize how much training and coaching my managers needed. I just assumed they'd figure it out." He created internal training playbooks and installed weekly structured 1:1s to train like a sports team.

- Coaching for a turnaround: The Opportunist, a rookie CEO I coached and is from my book, *The Rookie CEO, You Can't Make This Stuff Up*, overlooked training and providing coaching for his leadership team, and after several years the company's growth plateaued. We re-tooled the leadership team by upgrading all but one leader by installing the Top-grading method and Who method to hire A-players, and he brought in Vistage to help both himself and his leaders. We also implemented a scorecard system with SMART goals. The result was to break out of the plateau, experience new growth which lead to a successful exit, acquired by a great company.

Conclusion

Startups don't fail from lack of ideas. They fail when execution outpaces leadership maturity. If you want leverage, don't just hire people, develop them.

If you want scale, harvest your leaders who can lead through growth with you. The strongest CEOs don't just lead, they create leaders.

Bonus Section #2: The 90-day Growth Engine Challenge Framework

For the next 90 days and starting today, without a budget, without any excuses, and with your CEO commitment, implement these three rituals: track results, refine, repeat.

1. Host a thirty-minute Grow Talk with your key leaders.

- Once per month, assemble your leaders and experts to solve one real problem together.

- Rotate meeting leaders, but once you kick off, that shouldn't be you. The "Grow Talk" lead teaches something new. Make learning a ritual.

- Select one real business problem to solve or use as a teaching lesson.

- Measure effectiveness after the ninety-day pilot and discuss refinements after the 90 days.

- One option might be to create a shared library using Notion, Confluence, or some other platform.

2. Launch a Thirty-Minute Mentorship program

- Initiate your "buddy program" by pairing a leader with someone earlier in their career, ideally an individual contributor with a promising future. In a sports analogy, these are your top prospects! Disregard the prospect's title.

- Each pairing has one thirty-minute insight per session. This will drive a culture shift. It could be a company sponsored lunch, unless your team is remote, in which case you could deliver lunch to each.

3. Add an Insight "Power Up Minute" to team meetings.

- Create a logo or icon that signifies the "power-up" inside your company.

- At the start of every team meeting, have someone (rotate who shares) share one new insight (a new AI tool, a team or sales win, or a customer story; make it a learning moment at the beginning of every team meeting and keep it to three to five minutes).

- CEO goes first.

Log and track impact of your new programs from each session, win, or story using your platform. Your Growth Engine Tracker should include:

- Session recaps

- Quotes that provide value

- Insights gained

- Names of contributors

After the first 90-day Growth Engine Challenge, you'll have started your learning cultural engine that you can make a ritual or habit. Keep it going and growing. This program isn't just about training. It's about building leadership development muscles into your company's day-to-day operations.

Celebrate at an all-hands meeting, include updates in your company newsletter, and make your culture visible.

Here are my secrets for becoming the most confident and powerful CEO you can be while supercharging your leadership team and employees:

Secret #14: Great CEOs coach. But elite CEOs turn leadership development into a KPI. Assign each senior leader the responsibility and accountability to grow their teams. Make growth visible, measurable, and celebrated. Top CEOs don't just say, "our people are our greatest asset" because they visually prove it on an ongoing basis.

Chapter 15

Hiring Sales Leaders

Tom burned 9 months and blew four sales hires.

Tom's mistake? Assuming Sales VPs from top brand name companies would deliver revenues on day one. He figured that their plans and connections would instantly translate to deals. Tom leads a late-stage startup in the IT Services space and has tier one partners as part of his go-to-market strategy.

Much has been written about hiring sales leaders (VP, CRO) for a startup of any stage, especially when there is no sales team in place except for the CEO and COO themselves, both cofounders, who teamed up for the first few years.

The Mistake

When interviewing these sales leaders, each candidate was asked to create their first 90-to-100-day plan to create a minimum $1M pipeline.

Any sales leader candidate can create a 90-to-100-day plan with ease for an interview. There was one key element left out of the interview process: communicating it to the candidate that this plan will be part of their compensation plan, and they will be measured on it. Tom never told them this was the case until after they were hired full time. The sales leader was the only sales resource.

- Mistake #1: This disconnect in communication to the candidate is the primary mistake. It is a costly mistake when repeated four times in a matter of months!

- Mistake #2: To make matters worse, when you hire your first sales resource for your startup, hire producers, not senior leaders who need a team to execute under them.

The result? No new pipeline. No new revenue. No alignment.

Setting the Stage

Tom's interview playbook was solid. But his execution playbook did not exist. Tom assumed experience meant execution, but what was missing was the scrappiness needed at startups.

Candidates do their assignments as part of an interview process. The expectation is the exercise shows how they create plans, and how they might approach the challenge of the role. All senior sales leaders can create this type of plan easily.

When onboarding the new sales leader, Tom and his number two executive did a three hour "everything we do at the company presentation" and this was it along with their 90-to-100-day plan. Then they are cut loose. The first candidate suggested bringing on a marketing head to generate demand and leads for the sales leader and then hiring sales development reps to follow up on leads. This idea from the new sales leader was the traditional way senior sales leaders would execute and build their team. But it adds to cash burn rate without revenues and was never discussed in the interview process.

The Decision Process: "The Hidden Trap" The Ninety-Day Plan That Backfired

The candidates aced their plans but did not know they would be measured on it.

Furthermore, there was little to no support to achieve the goals of the candidates.

The trap? Tom hired for planning and strategy, but what was needed was prospecting. This is an example of cleverness over clarity. Tom thought he was clever, but he was never clear in his communications with the new sales leaders. His quote was, "I thought if they had a plan, they'd deliver pipeline." Tom later admitted, "Turns out, they needed a support team to even get started!"

The Results

When the first sales leader did not bring in any meetings after three months, he was terminated. The same thing happened with subsequent candidates who were hired (numbers two through four)! The same mistake should NEVER happen, but Tom did not learn from these mistakes. Just about nine months were lost as the hires were serially hired, and fired, one by one.

One sales leader did close one deal, funded by a partner, that was a trial with a big brand, but it did not move forward beyond the initial trial.

The sales solution ended up being that the marketer who was hired from candidate #1's recommendation added sales to her marketing leadership role and hired "newbie" sales development reps (SDRs) right out of school. Now, someone besides Tom and the CTO could do follow-up calls with prospects coming from email campaigns. It worked well.

In the second half of 2025, many companies are creating AI agents to emulate SDRs. These AI agents can manage the equivalent role 24/7 once the AI agent is trained. Thought provoking for many of you, no doubt.

How to Avoid This Mistake

The 90-to-100-day plan is a fine exercise as part of the interview process. But disclose to the candidate this is their plan for the first 90-to-100 days. Ask the candidate what resources they will need to achieve the plan, as part of the plan, and now you as CEO can decide if this candidate will fit the open role, the culture, and start with a high percentage chance to achieve success.

Better yet, hire a marketer to build brand and to create demand, hire a non-leader sales resource to work with the marketer, and build and perfect a repeatable sales process. Scale comes after the process is working. As revenue scales, you can add a sales leader.

Recovery and Moving Forward – the Fix that Actually Worked

The following months, the marketing head hired three newbie SDRs, and this structure and sales process were successful. Each SDR was onboarded by the marketing head, there was no 100-day plan, and they were trained to follow directions and follow up with prospects.

There were refinements, training, and development along the way for these new sales resources, but most of the team was intact to build a repeatable predictable sales and marketing process without having to pay huge salaries to sales leaders from large consulting firms.

The marketing head didn't just build demand, she built a repeatable system.

Conclusion

This mistake, made four times, is inexcusable and should never happen. Although the example is for sales leaders, this mistake applies to all leadership positions.

To all CEOs, especially first-time CEOs, A-list resumes don't build your revenue engine. Grit, fit, and follow-up do. You need implementers who can both strategize and execute while making stuff happen! Some call it "GSD" candidates and employees: "get stuff done" types with incredibly dedicated work ethics who are resourceful! True Grit!

Here is an **adaptable sales and marketing hiring roadmap for startups:**

- Founder-led sales and marketing: refine messaging, clear ICP, and overcoming objections.

- Hire a marketer: an executor to build demand and fill top of funnel.

- Add SDRs: handle lead follow-up and qualify prospects (AI is being used by some companies to fill this role).

- CEO closes deals until there is a predictable and repeatable process.

- Hire a sales leader to scale.

- Hire a marketing leader to scale and build strategy.

Secret #15: Never hire a VP of Sales before you've built a repeatable sales process. Your first sales hire should be a doer: someone who can prospect, pitch, and close; build demand first; then scale with leadership.

Chapter 16

Misreading Motivation: How the Wrong Move Breaks Trust

One bad idea can break trust overnight, disrupt company momentum, and even kill the company.

That's what happened to the Dealmaker. His intentions were good. His creativity unmatched. But his blind spot? Assuming all groups were motivated by the same thing. This one misguided move turned a technical delay into a leadership disaster. The Dealmaker was introduced in *"The Rookie CEO, You Can't Make This Stuff Up!"*

The Mistake

The Dealmaker believed a bold gesture would motivate the engineering team to hit an unreasonable delivery date.

It was a creative idea, but with significant drawbacks and risks. His plan? Roll in a wheelbarrow with $100,000 cash into a meeting and offer it as a bonus for delivering early. He thought this would light a fire but instead it burned trust with the founders.

Why was this such a costly mistake? Because motivation is personal. The Dealmaker assumed engineers think like sales teams. He never stopped to ask about what mattered to them. His blind spot of misreading motivation was the root cause of the disaster that followed.

Setting the Stage

The company came out of stealth mode through two tradeshows over a one-month period with a strong market position and created a buzz with the press, analysts, resellers, international integrators, and tier-one enterprise customers. The startup also won a "best of show" award. The product was not ready yet, but excitement was electric, and all team members were celebrating! Trade publications felt the company was front-page newsworthy.

Then came the painful news from development: there was a six-month delay due to a technical issue the team discovered in performance stress testing.

The company and products had been in beta with very large enterprise customers and partners. Ouch.

This delay stalled the momentum achieved before and at the two events. A piece of advice: before announcing your company and offerings publicly in a mind-blowing and expensive launch, hold tough-love meetings with the development and testing teams to ensure they are as close to 100% convinced the deliverable dates can be achieved and have mitigated risks.

The Decision Process

To the Dealmaker, this was life or death for the company's success. In this critical moment, he strongly felt it was necessary to deliver faster or lose all the beta customers and prospects already sold on the solution.

However, the Dealmaker had his own decision-making process which came from his sales point of view. He envisioned a dramatic scene by revealing stacks of dollar bills, rally cry to the engineers to deliver faster than their six-month delay, but he learned:

- Engineers care about solving problems, not stunts.

- Safety risks: large sums of cash could attract the wrong attention. Even the local police recommended not to do this.

- Most importantly, the perception : this move would signal distrust, pressure, and a lack of understanding of what drives the team.

When the idea was presented to the founders in the boardroom, their response was immediately shock and anger. "You don't trust us! You just don't believe us!" Those words landed like a sledgehammer. Trust was fractured forever and was unrecoverable for the Dealmaker.

The Results

Once trust is broken in a startup, recovery is rare. Word spread. Investors heard. The Dealmaker went from the key leader to a liability almost overnight.

Within a few months, he was out. His blind spot wasn't creativity, it was empathy. He didn't realize that a stunt could undo everything he'd worked so hard to build.

The company eventually hired a new CEO, changed products, market positioning, and tried hard to recover. This momentum was never regained, and the investors sold the IP and all assets.

How to Avoid This Mistake

Hindsight being twenty/twenty, the topic should have been discussed in an emergency meeting to explore every possible way to shorten the gap from that day to the new deliverable date. Bringing together the leaders, subject matter experts, and idea people can often close big gaps, but the Dealmaker did not take that approach at that time.

There may be other decision-process tools that CEOs can apply, but the Dealmaker used his own process. If you ever consider difficult life-changing decisions, you may want to look from new perspectives and use something else in addition to your own process.

Key takeaways:

- Know what motivates your team. Never assume.

- Ask questions before you act. Include all key leaders in these discussions.

- Applying pressure to your team without alignment creates resistance, not results.

- Consider the optics. Even well-intended gestures can be interpreted as distrust.

Recovery and Moving Forward

The Dealmaker learned the hard way that trust is a one-shot deal in a startup. He eventually started a new company, grew it steadily, and retired successfully. But he never forgot the cost of that misstep: misunderstanding motivation and breaking trust.

Conclusion

Leadership isn't just about great ideas. It's about understanding people. Motivation isn't universal, its personal. When in doubt, ask. Listen. Learn. Trust is the foundation of every team, and once it's gone, no wheelbarrow of cash can buy it back.

Secret #16: Motivation is personal. Don't assume cash moves everyone. As CEO, your job is to learn what drives each team, build trust with integrity, and lead with empathy. A wheelbarrow of cash can't buy trust, but it can shatter it.

Chapter 17

The Delegation Trap

"If I want it done right, I'll get it done myself!"

You may have heard this from your founder CEO.

It sounds noble. But it's a trap. It kills trust, teams, and time.

When I started coaching Greg, he had not taken a day off for eighteen months. He had grown his recurring revenue, but he was reaching a stress point because of his delegation syndrome. He rewrote sales decks, he reviewed every detail of the product design specifications and plan, changing what was already agreed to, and he took over calls that he "stopped into" just to see how things were going.

His leadership team was frustrated because they were quite capable, but he had to put his fingerprint on it. Often, he'd ask for a copy of a deck to review. He would work all night or weekend, and he would completely trash his team's work and replace it with his. Did he just not trust his team?

"Delegating feels like a disaster to me!" he told me one day when I asked why he overruled his team's work. He did not see what I saw, a classic founder blind spot: controlling micromanagement, draining his team's motivation, and lack of trust for some team members. The more often this happened, the less effective his team became, making the environment toxic for his leaders who were trying to do their job quite well. He did not realize it.

Greg was in a bind, as the company's success was on the line. The trust was gone.

The Mistake

There are two mistakes Greg made:

- Mistake #1: Greg believed it was faster to do it himself.

- Mistake #2: he stepped in late and loud (takeover)

Greg believed it was faster to do it all himself. Delegation felt risky, so he avoided it to stay in full control. Every time he took over, he was signaling to his team their work was not good enough. This is called, "The Takeover."

The "takeover" is when the CEO assigns someone from his team to handle a project that does not interest them at the time. The team member does a fantastic job maneuvering the project through the business development process. When the project rises to be one of the "hot" prospects or products, the CEO takes over now that it has high visibility. This happens in companies of all sizes, from startups to multimillion dollar multinational corporations.

In Greg's case, a lead came in from a tradeshow. We always prioritized leads that we spent a lot of time with, doing demos and answering questions from curious prospects, and we nurtured this lead until Greg stepped in to drive the project. The director of business development was not invited to any meetings after the "takeover" and was not given the commission he earned to get the deal as far as he did. This is not just bad form; it's a team killer. As a founder CEO, he should have partnered with the business development director rather than push him aside thanklessly. It appeared to be lack of trust from Greg.

A common fallacy among founders who can't let go easily: "No one can do it better than me."

The common founder result: You are teaching your team they can't be trusted. Once trust is gone, motivation follows and people often leave.

The Takeover Trap

CEOs don't mean to break trust. But this exact behavior does it every time.

My **takeover framework** is adaptable to many situations, but here it is:

- You assign a task that you don't care about (yet).

- The team member delivers without any drama.

- The initiative becomes "hot" or strategic high priority.

- The CEO moves the team member aside and takes it over himself.

- They disengage, lose motivation, credit, and trust.

Setting the Stage

As founder CEO, you lead sales, marketing, finance, product, and just about every decision made at the company in the early startup stages. That is the "founder mode." Over time, as the company grows, you should share the burden by hiring the right people. If you don't trust them, either coach them or move them out fast. Trust is the currency of delegation.

Owning it all can lead to you being overloaded and overwhelmed. Begin early on training your team so they'll know what goes into your decisions. Every decision, every fire drill, and every task flows through you. It feels like leadership, but it's an opportunity to educate and grow your team on your thought process. It allows you to build trust. You are still involved in the decisions, but over time, you can begin to delegate these decisions once full trust is earned on both sides.

You're proud of your work ethic. But the business is quietly suffocating under your need to be in the middle of everything, and this is why you should bring your cofounder and senior team into your day-to-day process. Don't clog workflows, bring your team into your process and you will not regret it.

Greg did not bring his team into his decision process. Thus, he paid a high price. When you are the hero in every story, no one else gets to grow.

The Decision Process

In Part 4 of this book, I share "Decision-Making" processes and provide powerful secrets and insights to frameworks for better decision-making. Delegation is a key part of the process. So why was it a struggle for Greg?

- Belief: He told himself no one else can do it right or fast enough.

- Bias: Greg convinced himself delegation was a timewaster. In reality, doing it all himself was the bottleneck.

- Fear: He feared letting go and making himself irrelevant.

- Control: He confused "accountability" with "ownership of every task."

Not all these points are true. Its ego disguised as efficiency. It's a quest for power and control. It's lack of trust of your team members.

The coaching conversation with Greg revealed bluntly that he was the problem. It was a hard pill for him to swallow. But he heard the conversation and, together, built a method for him to start the process of delegation and letting go of every decision. Greg needed to focus on what he, as CEO, was required to do, not what he felt he needed to do to massage his ego and maintain full control. If anyone was not capable of taking on responsibility, they would be removed from the key position.

We worked through an organizational structure where there were leaders who came to work every day committed to their business function and built a cross functional decision process. Keep in mind that there is no one solution that always solves this problem. Customize your solution to provide structured empowerment for your team.

Always be sure to monitor each situation and be ready to step back in if something looks to be not working. If your approach works, however, you will have a productive and motivated group of leaders.

The Results

From chaos to clarity: Greg's 90-day shift. It took about 90 days to create this new habit and see meaningful progress. We created scorecards for each key leader and subject matter expert. We defined expectations, decision process, and an expedited process to address one of the issues Greg had: speed. He wanted to clear open issues that he could solve immediately. Have you experienced the CEO who wants instant answers? Likely, yes.

Solid processes with all its details will facilitate the decisions needed and the leaders accountable to the team and CEO. What did Greg and the team learn? Here is their **ninety-day re-alignment framework:**

- Define the process.

- Align on the process.

- Create SMART goals and scorecards to eliminate ambiguity and blind spots.

- Re-engage the team.

- Removed Greg as the bottleneck.

- Publish the process and assign a process manager to own execution.

By the end of 90 days, Greg had a leadership team that was functioning, aligned, and respected. I helped coach Greg and his team through this process to deliver a repeatable system.

How to Avoid This Mistake

- Define the process, document the process, and assign owners.

- Set **clear expectations**; clarity is a critical success factor.

- Hold people accountable *by using scorecards to measure performance.*

- Create a delegation framework to include what will be delegated, who owns it, the checkpoints, the risks, and the potential roadblocks.

Delegation builds trust, capability, and culture. It's your force multiplier. Greg was able to listen and learn and trust his team over time. It took longer than 90 days to master, but the plan was a thirty-sixty-ninety-day roadmap, and he followed it. Success.

This was the secret to Greg's becoming more confident and powerful!

Recovery and Moving Forward

Greg needed coaching to let his team win. After a few months, he was back to "focusing on CEO-level priorities," even though he still asks many curious questions to feel more comfortable about delegation. His team knows that he will ask many questions, so he understands their approach and their path to the outcomes.

He has become curious, not controlling.

Conclusion

You can't scale unless you delegate. No company can achieve global dominance with the CEO stuck in every decision.

Delegation is a CEO superpower. It should not be a secret, but it is the secret to confidence and power as the CEO.

Six months after we started working together, Greg no longer felt the urge to "takeover" slides at 10:00 PM, and his calendar was under control. Although they were a small team, everyone had their scorecards and monitored them on a regular basis. Instead of slowing decisions down, it sped up the process, making everyone happy and motivated on the leadership team.

Everything seemed to be a great improvement over the older controlling Greg. The team was engaged, people helped and relied on each other, and bidirectional trust was born.

The culture shifted. Greg didn't lose control; he gained his leadership respect!

Secret #17: The best CEOs don't do it all. They build teams they trust, set clear expectations, and delegate with discipline. Delegation is not giving up control. It's how you scale leadership.

Chapter 18

The Price of Hiring Too Soon. It's all About Timing.

Rob Black, Founder and CEO of Fractional CISO, a bootstrapped startup company, learned the hard way that optimism doesn't pay salaries. Hiring ahead of revenue feels bold until cash starts to run out.

As many first-time CEOs discover, the excitement of growing their baby and scaling can lead to decisions that outpace revenue. These decisions that can have painful consequences. Rob's story is a classic example of what happens when you hire ahead of your growth and attempt to transition key responsibilities too quickly.

The Mistake

Rob's mistake was straightforward but costly. He hired three new employees: (1) one Virtual CISO (Chief Information-tion Security Officer), (2) a cybersecurity analyst, and (3) a salesperson. He expected that the company's growth would support them. In doing so, he was also trying to transition the sales process away from himself in founder-led sales mode and onto the new salesperson. However, the revenue didn't meet expectations, and Rob found himself in a position where he couldn't support the new hires. In Q2 of 2023, the hard decision was made to let them go. There is significant pain the first-time a rookie CEO must let people they hired go.

The transition from founder-led sales to hiring your first sales headcount is a tricky and much discussed topic in founder CEO discussion groups. It will continue to be a key discussion and decision point. Some experts believe the founder should lead all sales and marketing until "product (or service)-market-fit" is achieved. To complicate matters further, there is a debate about which comes first, marketing or sales. Rob's mistake was classic, however, and here is his complete story.

You'll note that, in this book, there are multiple examples of handing off founder-led sales too quickly. It's like giving your race car to a valet. They may know how to drive, but they don't know *your car*.

Setting the Stage

Fractional CISO was on a strong growth trajectory in 2022. Cybersecurity services were in high demand, and the company had comfortably expanded to fifteen employees. The team was starting to feel the pressure of that growth, and Rob was hearing consistent feedback about the need for more hands to address the business growth. There was an urgency to hire more staff, particularly someone to help with the flood of marketing-qualified leads. Rob made the call to bring on the three employees, confident that the company's growth would justify the decision.

The logic seemed sound. Based on past performance, 2023 looked promising, and Rob believed that transitioning away from founder-led sales would allow him to focus on scaling the business. But, as we know, business doesn't always follow projections.

The Decision Process

While the decision to hire wasn't "easy," Rob had grown the company steadily over the years and had reason to believe the pace of expansion would continue. Cybersecurity was booming, the team was asking for help, and the sales funnel seemed strong enough to justify the new hires. In Rob's mind, the best way forward was to bolster the team and delegate sales to a dedicated representative.

However, as many first-time CEOs learn, there's a critical distinction between founder-led sales and hiring a sales team. Founders often have deep relationships with customers and an intimate understanding of the company's product and services. Transitioning that knowledge to someone new takes time, and it's not always a smooth handoff.

Rob had the right intent, but the timing was off.

Here is a short **sales hiring checklist** to review and ask yourself before handing off sales:

- Is your sales process fully documented and repeatable?

- Are you hitting your consistent product-market-fit?

- Do you have enough inbound qualified leads to support a full-time sales rep?

- Are you, as CEO, still closing more than 80% of the deals personally?

The Result

By the second quarter of 2023, it became clear that growth wasn't keeping pace with expectations. Revenue lagged projections, and Fractional CISO was burning through cash faster than anticipated. Rob was faced with a harsh reality: The company wouldn't have enough money to pay staff by the end of the year if they continued down the same path.

The decision to let the three employees go was painful. Reductions-in-force (RIFs) always shake the confidence of a team. It causes doubt about the company's future and leads to a dip in morale as employees wonder if they'll be next. For Rob, the experience was especially difficult because he had to undo a decision that was meant to propel the company forward. Instead, it had the opposite effect, slowing growth and creating uncertainty.

How to Avoid This Mistake

Hindsight often reveals the clearest path forward, and Rob can now point to two key things he would do differently. First, he wouldn't hire ahead of real revenue. In a small company, the margin for error is slim, and bringing on new employees before you have the revenue to support them is a bad idea.

Second, Rob emphasizes the challenge with the transition out of founder-led sales. Handing over the sales process should happen after the sales process is built, proven, and is ready to scale. And revenue warrants the sales hire.

Here are a few ideas to determine new sales headcount:

- Connect new headcount to actual revenue, not projections.

- Transition out of founder-led sales slowly, usually over three to four quarters.

- Create a cash buffer before hiring the new roles.

- Clarify ramp-up expectations for any sales hire. No one can replicate founder-passion or trust on day one.

Recovery and Moving Forward

Despite the setback, Fractional CISO managed to recover. The reduction-in-force was a tough but necessary move to keep the company afloat. Rob had to jump back into sales himself until the third quarter of 2023, when performance exceeded expectations and the company was back on the growth train.

Fractional CISO was able to rehire one of the three employees they had let go earlier. It was a bittersweet victory, but one that showed the team's ability to adapt and recover from the mistake.

Conclusion

Rob Black's story shares the dangers of hiring ahead of revenue and the complexities of transitioning out of founder-led sales. Many first-time CEOs find themselves in similar situations, but Rob's experience highlights two critical lessons: Always tie new hires to actual revenue and be patient when handing off key responsibilities. Patience is not always common in type-A, first-time CEOs!

About Rob Black

Rob worked with me in the early 2000s on the same product management team in a larger company. Although that was earlier in his career, it was obvious to me he had a terrific future ahead, and the decisions he made would shape his path forward. As his boss I was pleased to learn later that he was influenced by my leadership, and his success proved he made the right decisions.

Secret #18: Do not hire ahead of revenue. Hire based on revenue. Growth must be managed carefully, and scaling too fast can lead to setbacks that take years to recover from. But, with the right mindset, a willingness to make difficult and painful decisions, and a focus on recovery, it's possible to bounce back and build a stronger company for the future.

Part 4
Decision-Making

Chapter 19

CEO Decision-Making Frameworks

CEOs aren't measured by what they *intend*. They're measured by their decisions. Not just *what* they decide, but *how* they decide.

This chapter gives you a decision-making operating system. Every mistake you have read about in this book so far started with a faulty process.

We will explore the decision-making process in detail. Buckle up, as it's a wild ride!

Your leadership legacy, team trust, board confidence, and business direction are all rooted in how you make decisions. From whom to hire and promote, what to build, how to position your company, when to pivot, or where to invest your time and capital, every one of those moments stems from a decision. And how you make them is often more important than the decision itself.

The Mistake: Not Knowing Your Own Decision Process

Many CEOs lead without a clear understanding of how they make decisions. I have written about the CEO's decision-making process previously, and my belief is that we all have a process, even if it's just the way we operate based on our backgrounds, philosophy, and leadership style. It's our mindset.

As CEO, document your process, improve your process based on what we discuss in the coming sections, and consider creating your personal AI assistant to help guide you on an ongoing basis.

Setting the Stage

We often talk about what decisions the CEO made, but not enough about *how* they were made. That "how" determines everything. Whether it's:

- A rushed auto-decision that lacked key inputs and did not form a basis for decisions yet.

- A prolonged, over-analyzed choice that paralyzed the team.

- A politically motivated choice that satisfied no one.

Your company deserves better.

The Simple Decisions: Your Auto-Process

We all have a built-in auto-process for low-stakes, fast-moving decisions. These quickly made decisions with minimal data are grounded in your values, instincts, and experience. Whether conscious or unconscious, this framework serves a critical purpose: *speed.*

I describe this as:

- **Speed:** Time kills opportunities.

- **Facts:** Grab "just enough" accurate data.

- **Impact Questions:** Who/what will this affect? Is this reversible?

- **Check-in:** Gut "yes" or "no." (Don't make "gut" decisions without facts and impact considered.)

- **Action:** Do it now.

As CEO, you likely make hundreds of these decisions a week. They can be about meetings, new hires, spending, messaging, or product tweaks. Your auto-decision framework can create trust, clarity, and agility. Share with your team your process.

However, when the stakes are high, use a different process.

The Hard Decisions: Your Deliberate Process

Your framework must change when the decision involves risk, ethics, layoffs, executive hires, M&A (merger and acquisition), or anything irreversible. CEOs often rush their decisions when they should reflect, or stall when they must collect more accurate facts and consider trade-offs. The wrong decision can lead to mistakes that could severely impact your company, as you can see from stories shared by CEOs in this book.

My Six-Step "Fast-6 Decision Framework"

1. **Name the problem.** Not symptoms; the root cause.

2. **Collect clean data.** Quantitative and qualitative.

3. **Select voices.** Choose three to five inputs max. People who matter.

4. **Run simulations.** "What if" each outcome.

5. **Set a decision deadline.** Without a date, it's just discussion.

6. **Own it. Communicate it.** Share the why, not just the what.

CEO Decision Frameworks in Practice

In CEO interviews across my CEO Success Series and IT-EXPO panels, leaders consistently pointed out that their decisions shaped outcomes.

- **The Opportunist** used a hiring framework built from Topgrading plus the Who method to upgrade his leadership team to A-players.

- **Robert** struggled with speed-vs.-readiness tradeoffs and learned the value of team alignment pre-decision.

- **KG (Kevin Gaither)** admitted one of his biggest failures was silence in the face of misconduct (not making a real-time decision).

Whether they acted too quickly or hesitated too long, the gap was always in their framework. All addressed their process and improved their outcomes in the future.

Three CEO Decision Frameworks You Should Know

Visionary CEOs build their muscle on proven frameworks. Here are three frameworks widely used by top-performing leaders:

1. OODA Loop (Observe, Orient, Decide, Act)

- Developed by U.S. Air Force strategist John Boyd. Used by CEOs in dynamic, competitive environments, for tactical decisions.

- Focuses on agility: gather data (observe), understand context (orient), make the call (decide), take action (act), then loop.

- Jamie Dimon, Chairman and CEO of JP Morgan Chase uses OODA on. Regular basis.

2. First Principles Thinking

- Break down complex problems into short blocks.

- Avoid analogy traps, which can lead to questioning assumptions and innovation under pressure.

- Excellent for breakthrough innovation and solving difficult problems.

- Elon Musk, CEO of Tesla and SpaceX, uses First Principles Thinking.

- Jeff Bezos, Founder and former CEO of Amazon, encourages this framework.

- Reed Hastings, Cofounder and CEO of Netflix hired First Principle thinkers and encourages its use.

3. RAPID Framework (Recommend, Agree, Perform, Input, Decide)

- Developed by Bain & Company. This framework clarifies roles in decision-making.

- Prevents bottlenecks by aligning who does what in each part of the decision.

- This proprietary process has been implemented in Bain's client base across industries including global entertainment companies, companies in digital transformation phases, large enterprises with complex cross functional decisions and is widely.

4. There are two more popular task-focused frameworks, but I won't expand on them here: Eisenhower Matrix (primarily for tasks and priorities) and Pareto Principle (primarily for resource optimization).

Visionary CEOs don't blindly adopt frameworks; they adapt them for their purposes.

How to Avoid the Decision-Making Trap

- Know when you're in auto-mode. And when you shouldn't be.

- Map your process. Diagram it on a whiteboard and share it with your leadership team. This may help align your leadership team.

- Use a Decision Journal. Document the logic, inputs, timeframe, and outcomes. Over time, your process will get sharper. Create a custom GPT/AI Agent that helps you collect decision data points and refines your decision processes.

- Create decision tiers. Your auto-process will discover and define when you make the decision without collaborating with your team.

Recovery and Moving Forward

CEOs can usually recover from bad decisions. There are ways to execute, but each is unique to the individual CEO. Here are some tips to recover with your team and rebuild trust:

- Transparently and publicly, admit that your decision could have been handled differently.

- Apologize, clarify, and rebuild with your team.

- Review, document, and revise your process.

And remember: *Do not make the same mistake again!*

Here is a simple **reference chart** *to help guide your* **decision process** *stack:*

Decision Type	Process Used	Team Involvement
Fast action, tactical	Auto-process	No
High risk, strategic	Deliberate "Fast-6" Step	Yes
Team impacting	RAPID or OODA	Select team members

Conclusion

Do you have your own decision stack yet? Is it documented or in your head? Here is an adaptable method to create your personal decision stack:

- What are your top three recurring decision types?

- Which are auto? ("fast" decisions)

- Who are your go-to team members in each case?

- What's your time-to-decision metric for each type?

- What feedback loop exists to improve it?

Once you create your own stack, apply to your new habit and ritual creation.

- Every decision impacts the company. Speed matters, but process wins, especially for difficult more complex decisions.

- Document key decisions and outcomes.

- Create your personal decision-making framework.

- Include your team for the difficult decision process. Coach when necessary.

- Use accurate inputs, not opinions from others.

- Own your decision style and know when to change it.

- Learn and adapt frameworks like OODA, First Principles, RAPID, or other to your decision process framework. Revisit quarterly.

Secret #19: Your decision process is your CEO operating system. If you don't define it, it will define you. The best CEOs lead with clarity, not ambiguity, with every choice. They lead from the front. Lead with confidence, not chaos. Lead with decisions, not delays.

The result? Your decisions define your destiny. Lead with process, not guesswork. You will lead with confidence and power!

Chapter 20

Caught With a Floundering Pipeline?

As CEO, you may never realize the pipeline is slowing down, until the cash stops flowing.

"We had a full client roster. The team was humming. The machine was running. Then, the pipeline went dry."

That's how Adam Helweh, the founder and CEO of Secret Sushi, a Silicon Valley-based marketing agency, learned a hard lesson about sales that many first-time CEOs overlook.

In fact, this situation could happen to any CEO who overlooks the sales process and mismanages the pipeline progress. In the hustle and bustle of running a growing business, Adam took his foot off the gas when it came to maintaining a strong sales pipeline. He became comfortable fixing other inefficiencies and was late to address the sales pipeline slowdown. It was a mistake that took him by surprise but, over the long term, he was able to be a stronger CEO and leader.

The Mistake Summary

Adam's mistake was waiting too long to reinvest his time into building a reliable and growing sales pipeline. As his business grew, Secret Sushi's operations, team, and financials were running smoothly. Everything was working like a well-oiled machine. Adam had stepped back from many day-to-day tasks, enjoying the freedom that came from finally having a full roster of customers and a strong team to manage operations.

Delegating to your trusted sales leader does not mean ignoring your pipeline numbers. As CEO, you own the system, even though you have delegated operations of the day-to-day.

Adam soon realized that the agency's growth was heavily reliant on word-of-mouth referrals, an unpredictable and unsustainable source of new business. With all the other pieces in place, Adam needed to step into the sales role himself to secure a steady stream of clients. But, by the time he recognized this, the warning signs were already there, as clients were starting to churn, and the sales pipeline wasn't growing fast enough to keep up. There was an unforeseen impact on his team's morale and stress levels.

Adam didn't *ignore* the pipeline. He *assumed* success meant it would take care of itself. The mistake wasn't laziness. It was false confidence from a calm mindset.

Setting the Stage

Secret Sushi had spent years refining its processes, building a solid team, and improving financial planning. As the company grew, Adam fell into the trap many CEOs do: he got comfortable. He took his eyes off the ball, because his team was thriving, customers were happy, and the business felt stable.

When clients unexpectedly terminated services due to the economy, Adam was blindsided.

The Decision Process

At the time, everything about the business seemed strong. With a roster of loyal, recurring customers, Adam felt he had bought himself some time to focus on other areas. He relied on word-of-mouth for new business, a strategy that had worked well in the early stages of growth. However, as the agency matured, it became clear that word-of-mouth alone wouldn't sustain them in the long run. Sales needed more focus, and Adam, as the founder and CEO, needed to drive it. Adam felt he was best at sales, and he needed to jump back in fully to right the ship.

The Mistake

Adam admits he waited too long to take action to bolster the sales pipeline. Their contracts with clients were month-to-month after an initial three-month period, and while clients often stayed with Secret Sushi for a year or longer, there was always a risk of sudden attrition.

Clients left for reasons outside of Secret Sushi's control. Adam suddenly realized he hadn't built a sales pipeline to offset unexpected losses.

We have similar mistakes in this book where CEOs were leading and things were working smoothly, but unexpected market conditions changed the entire business.

The markets are dynamic, and overnight, the stock market can fall anywhere in the world, supply chains can be impacted by several outside events, and you have no fallback plans. Like Gary Lee's Plan B ideas, outside events can have a major business impact.

The Results

The sudden drop in revenue had a noticeable impact on Secret Sushi's finances and morale. Adam's team, accustomed to transparency, was aware of the challenges which put additional emotional pressure on everyone. They had to cut back business expenses and make sacrifices to give themselves time to rebuild the sales pipeline. Adam took a temporary pay cut, and the newest hire's hours were reduced to a minimum to keep her engaged until they could ramp up again.

How to Avoid This Mistake

Looking back, Adam knows he should have started building the sales pipeline earlier. Relying solely on word-of-mouth, while successful in the past, was not a sustainable long-term strategy. Adam realized that sales, especially in the marketing agency world, doesn't work like a light switch. It takes time to build momentum. A sustainable sales machine doesn't turn on overnight, and Adam's failure to recognize this early enough led to the financial strain they faced. In hindsight, he would have invested more effort into sales much sooner. Adam now understands the importance of anticipating client attrition and planning for it well in advance. He acknowledges that building a sales pipeline is a process, not an event, and he should have started the engine long before it became a necessity.

Here is a quick checklist that may help guide you to not make a similar mistake:

- Review your pipeline weekly or monthly.

- Build at least three lead channels; before you need them.

- Never rely on referrals as your primary lead source.

- Schedule time weekly for strategic selling, making time on your calendar.

- Build churn rates into your forecast.

Recovery and Moving Forward

Recovery didn't happen overnight, and as of the time of this writing, Secret Sushi is still in the process of rebuilding its pipeline. However, Adam's leadership and his team's culture of trust and transparency allowed them to adapt. They took a conservative approach to finances, forecasting new revenue with caution and cutting operational costs wherever possible. Adam and his COO took pay cuts to shield the rest of the team from the financial impact.

Secret Sushi also invested in multiple sales channels to diversify their lead generation efforts. Deals in his market can take months from lead to close. The remodeling of his sales machine paid off. Adam's more frequent financial reviews, along with a focus on long-term business, made his company healthier.

Conclusion

Adam Helweh's story is a sharp reminder for any CEO, especially those running service-based businesses. Growth isn't just about your team or your delivery. It's about keeping the sales engine running even when things feel steady.

Here's the truth: If you're not thinking about your pipeline until the pressure hits by surprise, you've waited too long. Sales is a CEO habit. Hitting a panic button is not good for the company.

Sales momentum doesn't build itself. It takes time. You can't just flip a switch when a big client leaves, or a deal falls through. If you don't have something already in motion, you're stuck playing catch-up, and that's where companies get into trouble.

Here is a mini framework to operate. By:

- Weekly forecast

- Monthly review vs. forecast

- Quarterly reset, if necessary

Suggestion: Never go more than five (5) business days without taking a snapshot of your pipeline.

Adam's experience shows us the importance of being ready, not reactive. But it also proves something bigger: When you're honest, lead with clarity, and make the tough calls, there's always a way forward.

Secret #20: Your sales pipeline is not a fire drill; it's a discipline! As CEO, you should never take your eyeballs off revenue generation. It's your company lifeblood that drives all other decisions. There is never a time when you should let your guard down. Be prepared and accountable, and lead with confidence and power!

Chapter 21

Gut Instincts or Data-Driven Decisions?

Every CEO hits this crossroads: Your gut says one thing, the data says another. Which do you trust?

Some swear by the gut. Others say, "If it's not in the numbers, it's not real."

The truth? The best CEOs know it's a formula that combines their gut and the data.

The Mistake: Letting Emotion Lead Without Evidence

The Opportunist, introduced in The Rookie CEO, You Can't Make This Stuff Up! ran his company mostly by instinct, except for his balance sheet.

His mistake breaks down into these three issues:

- No structured hiring process.

- Decisions made on feeling, not performance or proof points.

- Ignoring his team's input broke trust and stalled growth.

If you are more of a "gut feeling" CEO, the gut is just an advisor to you. Balance this with real data and what your team sees and tells you or it's just a blind spot.

He'd built a good team and had several early wins, but his hiring and firing process was inconsistent. If he interviewed you and liked you, you got an offer on the spot. If you were an employee and something felt off, even if you were performing, you were out.

He once ruled out a high-performing customer success leader because he "didn't vibe" with him. No performance issues. The interview team wanted to hire this candidate. His "gut" said there is no way he can work for me.

He also hired another customer success leader because he liked the way he "sounded" in the interview process. As it turned out, the guy had zero client-facing skills or capabilities and demotivated the team in less than 90 days.

He had a mess on his hands: burned bridges, a rattled team, and no repeatable hiring process. The company hit a plateau because of these three impactful issues.

When the chaos became obvious and predictable, he asked for help. That one decision changed his mindset and his company in a positive way forever.

Setting the Stage

In the early days of a company, founders rely on instinct and referrals. There's often not enough data. No clean dashboards. No HR systems. Decisions come fast and from the gut. Speed and "feelings" rule the mind.

But as the company grows, and as the stakes rise, that same instinct-only model becomes dangerous. Why?

Because gut instinct is shaped by emotion, ego, bias, and experience. And while that's not always bad, it's incomplete.

Especially when:

- You're hiring executives and leaders.

- You're cutting budgets.

- You're deciding to shut down or pivot on a product line.

- You're trying to reorganize a team that's already stretched thin.

In these moments, data helps you separate signal from noise.

The Decision Process

The Opportunist had a process that did not analyze the data to make made decisions. It relied mostly on his "gut" reaction.

Coaching the Opportunist: we created a simple custom framework:

1. Decision Type: Implement SMART goals using a spreadsheet and a scoring system.

2. Available Data or Creating Data: Business operations type of situations produce data, and the leaders need to track and monitor; for other decisions, the leadership teams discuss the issues and create a scoring system, and a designated scorekeeper maintains the spreadsheet and scores.

3. Bias Check: What's driving your emotion right now?

4. Gut Signal: What is your instinct saying, and why?

5. Data Direction: What are the metrics or inputs pointing to (from Step 2)?

6. Stakeholder Input: Trade-off discussions based on team input, concerns, and data as it relates to their role.

7. Make the Call. Document It. Customize for your company.

"Gut-driven" CEOs dislike this system approach at first. As the Opportunist stated, "It slowed me down, but it saved us." But, three months later, his decision quality went up, his leadership team more efficient, and performance improved across the board. It significantly helped the company culture and prepared the company for acquisition. We didn't remove gut. We gave it a reality check.

The Results

Once a scoring system was in place and applied, and the emotions were removed, the results were:

- Hiring better talent, because the team used interview scorecards and discussed details from the interviews.

- No more reactive organizational changes; all changes were based on strategic restructuring based on available data.

- He built trust across the leadership team, because decisions felt fair, thoughtful, and explainable.

Gut still played a role. But it was no longer the only voice in the room.

How to Avoid This Mistake

- Separate urgency from importance. Fast decisions don't have to be reckless.

- Use a simple decision document. Make a one-pager with description, desired outcomes, choices, scores based on possible choices, what data supports the choices, what risks exist, and what are risk mitigations, and who's involved.

- Create a bias checklist. Ask yourself (and the team if applicable): Is this emotion, fear, ego, or intuition? Name it before you act on it.

- Bring your team in. Let them poke holes based on discussions. Take appropriate actions.

- Trust your gut more when the data is thin. But trust data more when lives, livelihoods, or major capital are on the line.

Here is a simple adoptable decision document in a bulleted format. You should create a simple guide for any complex decision. It's the GIPD Model – Gut Instinct Plus Data Model. Once you start using this model, it will become second nature.

Sample GIPD Decision Framework, One-Pager Format:

- **Decision:** Hire new VP of Marketing

- **Desired Outcome:** Drive 30% pipeline growth in two quarters

  - **Options Considered:** Internal promotion vs. external hire

  - **Scoring Criteria:** Team fit, ICP knowledge, execution history

  - **Supporting Data:** Interview scorecards, references, prior pipeline stats

  - **Risks:** Culture misfit, delay in ramp-up

  - **Mitigations:** 30-60-90 day scorecard, weekly review

  - **Decision Owner:** CEO

You can adapt this framework to any complex decision: hiring, pricing changes, product pivots, or layoffs. It brings structure and clarity to what would otherwise feel chaotic.

Recovery and Moving Forward

The Opportunist became a better CEO not because he became "less emotional," but because he became more self-aware.

He still used his gut, but now he had tools and inputs to test it against.

He used to say, "I go with my gut." Now he says, "I go with my gut, then make sure the numbers don't call me a liar."

That mindset shift changed his company forever.

Conclusion

CEOs don't have the luxury of always being right. But they do have the responsibility to be rigorous.

Gut instincts are fast, human, and useful. But when they're left unchecked, they can become blind spots.

Your goal? Blend intuition with information. Lead with courage but decide with clarity.

The best CEOs aren't gut-driven or data-driven. They're *decision driven.*

Secret #21: The best CEOs are not gut-driven or data driven, they are decision-driven! Make it a habit to test your instincts against primary information and data. Then you can make the call with confidence and power. Seat-of-the-pants decision-making is for amateurs, not top-notch CEOs.

Chapter 22

Analysis Paralysis and Delayed Decision-Making

Every CEO faces this moment: when a promising new idea meets real-world constraints.

Resources are tight. Priorities compete and on plan. Risks feel high. The decision gets delayed.

But, while analysis is necessary, delay can become dangerous. This chapter dives into what happens when decision-making turns into decision-avoiding. Pay attention as this is more common than you think.

Let me reintroduce "the General" from my first book, *The Rookie CEO, You Can't Make This Stuff Up!* He was a thoughtful leader with decades of experience, a strong command of operations, and an eye for detail. He was methodical and precise. And when it came to one of the most significant product expansion opportunities his company ever had, he chose to delay his decision to proceed rather than upset the development team with priority changes. Had he made the decision to change priorities, it would have considerably impacted shorter-term projects with already projected revenue.

The Mistake: Waiting Too Long to Decide

The General delayed making a critical decision on launching a new business offering. His best salespeople were vocal advocates. The reseller channel was actively requesting it. Customer demand was evident. He had data. He had internal support. But he hesitated.

His reason? Capacity. The development team was small and already over-committed with feature requests. Prioritization was hard. Every project mattered. And rather than make the hard call, he chose to ask for more analysis, more modelling, and more patience. It wasn't a no. But it wasn't a yes. He took a "no decision" stance. This silence can kill momentum faster than a bad decision.

Setting the Stage

The idea was sound. The market was ready. The channel was hungry. But the internal team was at a breaking point. And, without clear prioritization from the top, nothing moved.

Over time, frustration grew. Salespeople stopped asking. The project stayed on ice, even though one champion kept responding to the next level of analysis with competitive updates and more business model details.

The Decision Process

The General believed in making data-driven, well-considered decisions. That's not a flaw. But, in this case, the mistake wasn't in the care, it was in the lack of *communication*. No one (outside of a two-person inner circle) knew where the decision stood. He requested analysis repeatedly but didn't share intent, direction, or any clear criteria for decision-making.

It was like asking for directions without saying where you are heading.

What makes this so common is the *in-between* space many CEOs get trapped in: the belief that more data will clarify the answer. But the data already told the story.

He had:

- Customer demand
- Sales and channel enthusiasm
- A market opportunity window
- Internal roadblocks

What he lacked was a framework for making the call and a willingness to own the trade-offs publicly. He never did clarify what was missing for him to make a definitive decision.

One solution could have been a "Decision Readiness Scorecard" or similar, with the team advocates answering these questions:

- Initiative or product owner identified and assigned?

- Criteria to invest vs. feature development?

- Market update, size, and opportunity?

- Deadline or timeline?

- Opportunity costs?

The Results: The Good, the Bad, and the Ugly

The Good: When the decision was finally made, three years later, the product did launch. And it performed well. Customers adopted it. The channel re-engaged. It ultimately helped stabilize growth.

The Bad: By the time it launched, competitors had already stepped in. What could have been a first-mover advantage became a late-stage response. The team felt burned out from the whiplash of stop-start priorities. There was significant lost revenue opportunity.

The Ugly: The biggest damage was internal. Trust in leadership took a hit. Some people moved on. Some channel partners never came back. And much of the leadership team felt excluded from a decision that affected everyone.

Most damaging of all? The General never acknowledged the delay as a mistake. To him, the timing was finally right. To the company, the cost was real.

How to Avoid This Mistake:

- **Define a decision date.** Don't leave it open-ended. Set a timeline and work toward it.

- **Clarify your criteria.** What conditions must be true for a yes? What are the deal-breakers?

- **Communicate status.** Silence signals inaction. Keep stakeholders informed, even if the answer is "not yet."

- **Prioritize with courage.** No dev team can do everything. Your job is to choose.

- **Accept imperfect information.** Waiting for perfect data is waiting forever.

Recovery and Moving Forward

To his credit, the General did eventually approve the new offering. He committed the resources. He supported the launch. But the delay had a cost.

What could have been a celebrated internal win became a "finally" moment.

Future decisions were made with more transparency. He began using a prioritization framework and involved his leadership team earlier. He totally understands how the team interprets his approach.

Conclusion

The best CEOs don't delay without communications of curiosity. They collect all the readiness scorecard data. Align the team. Decide, based on their decision framework. Then lean into it. Be transparent about why to delay or what information is needed to move forward.

Secret #22: Delaying a decision isn't always the worst choice. But doing so without transparency, prioritization, and a clear end point *is*. CEOs must learn to act with confidence, even when all the data isn't in. The job isn't just to make the right decision, it's also to make the decision right. That is leading with confidence and power.

Chapter 23

Crisis Management

Dear CEO, your CFO, or VP of Finance can be your best friend or your worst enemy.

This chapter shares a real story about a first-time CEO who made two deadly mistakes. One "bad apple" CFO, and one broken system, led to a $5M embezzlement, a company shutdown, and a lesson no CEO should ever forget.

There is a myriad of books that discuss crisis management and leadership, but for our purposes, I will share one story that has multiple parts to it, and all driven from a "bad apple" CFO. It's a heads-up example of why the CEO must take ownership of every dollar that goes out of the company.

Mismanaged money, and lack of oversight of your CFO or VP of Finance, can lead to losses that the company cannot recover from. This is a real example from a few years ago but this situation can easily happen anytime.

The Mistake

The Dealmaker (from Chapter 16) returns in this story. This time, he is facing a financial crisis brewing behind the scenes and out of sight.

The Dealmaker was responsible for cash flow and cash in the bank, which was significant series B cash, well over $20M. There are two mistakes in this "crisis" chapter:

1. Signature authority

2. Lack of cash flow and spending oversight

The signature authority is aligned with delegation and trust from the CEO to whichever executive is chosen to be the signer of invoices being paid out. We had a two-level process where smaller invoices were signed off by the CFO, and the CEO never saw the amounts or who was being paid. Larger invoices would require the Dealmaker's signature. Reconciliation was sometimes done, even in preparation for board meetings where updated quarterly data was shared.

The second mistake was related to the first. Since the "bad apple" CFO had signature authority, he was able to create offshore accounts that no one else knew about. He kept these fake invoices for "services rendered" to the amounts he could sign off on and paid himself without anyone's knowledge except the controller who worked for him and never questioned anything.

Can you see what's coming yet?

Setting the Stage

Cash was disappearing, but the amounts were small enough for a while that no one could figure out anything was wrong. As CEO, cash and the financials are your responsibility. You should have a system to track run rate and cash available at any point in time. The Dealmaker trusted his CFO and did not see it or track it on his terms. No one had oversight accountability and the CFO knew it.

Month by month, the cash was leaving the premise, and only the CFO knew what was spent and where it was going. The smaller amounts were adding up.

Senior team members became aware that the CFO was attempting to orchestrate the Dealmaker's removal and replacement with his own ally. This represented a crisis in the making. When the CFO approached other executives to join his coup, he was turned away.

The Decision Process

The Dealmaker was warned about this motion, and that he should fire the CFO. But since the company was in the middle of raising series C funding, he felt that couldn't afford to terminate the CFO. Investors would not be comfortable with a leadership termination so close to a funding round.

Keep in mind, this was a closed set of discussions that no one else knew about. The Dealmaker was in a very difficult position with all the activity in motion.

The Results

Some executives left the company and turned in their corporate credit cards. Everyone was asked to use personal credit cards to pay for company expenses and get reimbursed. This was a change. There were only five cards with a limit on each card.

Two months later, the bank called the executives that left that they were in arrears and owed them the maximum amount. All had to prove to the bank they left the company and no longer had access to the credit cards.

But, by these bank calls, the Dealmaker was gone. An outside CEO was brought in, and he brought a consultant in-house to help. As we all know, it is a small world. The consultant used to work with an executive at a previous company, saw his signature on a piece of memorabilia, and called him.

Being under a non-disclosure agreement, the executive had to be careful what he told him, but was able to point the consultant in the right direction that uncovered the following:

- All five credit cards that were supposedly taken out of service were maxed out and not being paid.

- In reviewing accounts payable, several offshore fake accounts were determined to be receiving monthly payments authorized by the CFO.

- All fake accounts were owned by the CFO via an alias.

- Five million dollars were drained from the bank account.

It all started with one simple, but fatal, decision: The Dealmaker gave up signature authority.

How to Avoid This Mistake and How CEOs Can Stop This Before It Starts

These two mistakes are interrelated. They caused a corporate and investor crisis that ended being unrecoverable. I wrote about the signature authority in my first book, *The Rookie CEO, You Can't Make This Stuff Up!* and received one review that said, "No CEO would ever make the signature authority mistake!" It would seem obvious, but I have a client from my first book lead magnet who hired me as an advisor and told me this was an eye-opener for him. Since reading my book, he has had some people want to wrestle ownership of signature authority from him. No way, he said, after learning about this story.

First-time CEOs and startup CEOs: Never give up signature authority, even for small purchases. Know and track where every dollar is being spent. For mid-sized and larger companies, and more experienced CEOs who delegate signature authority, create a standard budget tracking mechanism to review every dollar spent. These days, automation can assist you in tracking expenditures and look for anomalies. Thank you, AI!

What is difficult is that founders and investors will not usually admit they were embezzled from, because it is poor crisis management and poor form for the CEO who was in charge at the time and the board who lost oversight.

These two mistakes, giving up signature authority and failing to track spending, are almost always preventable. Here is how to keep your company protected:

Bonus Protection: The Financial Oversight Decision Framework

Every CEO who delegates any level of signature authority should use this one-page framework. The framework includes:

- Who holds what authority and what are the escalation thresholds

- Approval workflows and exceptions

- Audit cadence and reconciliation points

- AI/automation tools for alerts or pattern detection

- Contingency plan if oversight fails

This keeps you in control and keeps bad actors from slipping through the cracks. You could create a corporate oversight committee that reviews all payments and approvals and meets once per quarter or on some cadence.

Recovery and Moving Forward

This company ultimately shut down. The technology was sold to the series B corporate investor, and the venture investors got a small piece back as the company was dissolved. This was a serious mistake that manifested itself later due to a "bad apple" CFO, an unlikely scenario.

Conclusion

Cash is king. Protect the company. Know your numbers. Revenue, costs, margins, suppliers, customers, service providers, and do not let a CFO, full time or part-time fractional, controller, or any finance person take the keys away from you. The CEO's number one role is keeping the company afloat. Execute this correctly to lead with confidence and power.

Secret #23: Never give up full signature authority. If you do delegate, create a real-time method to know how every dollar was spent as well as where and for what. You, as CEO, are accountable.

Part 5
Ethical and Integrity

Chapter 24

The Illusion of Success: Elizabeth Holmes and the Fall of Theranos

The story of Elizabeth Holmes and Theranos has a high-profile history, with multiple movies and mini-series dedicated to it. I have included it here as a crucial case study for CEOs, offering valuable insights on navigating and recovering from similar challenges.

Elizabeth Holmes was once the princess of Silicon Valley. She was a young, ambitious female entrepreneur. She founded Theranos to revolutionize healthcare by making blood testing faster, cheaper, and more accessible in drugstore chains using just a single drop of blood.

Theranos had achieved a valuation of nine billion dollars, but it lacked a real backbone to serve the public. It was a crazy time. Holmes's mistake was deliberately misleading investors, partners, and the public about the device the company had developed. This allowed her to create a facade of a next-generation healthcare company and become a billionaire. Instead, it led to one of the largest company collapses in history!

The Mistake

Elizabeth Holmes made several critical mistakes as CEO of Theranos, but lack of integrity was at the top of the list.

Overpromising a New Product:

Holmes aggressively marketed Theranos's blood-testing technology before it was validated to work correctly. The company claimed its device, the Edison, could run hundreds of tests on just a finger-prick of blood, a claim that was never true, even though it was her bold vision.

Creating a Culture of Fear and Secrecy:

Holmes fostered a toxic work environment where employees were siloed and discouraged from sharing information. Naysayers were silenced through intimidation and legal threats, preventing the company from addressing its technological failures.

Lies, Lies, and More Lies to Investors and Partners:

Holmes consistently lied to everyone she wanted to both secure funding from and partner with.

Holmes Had No Guardrails or Boundaries:

Her journey was nothing more than continued lies, keeping nearly everyone except her from knowing that the product vision was not viable.

Setting the Stage

Holmes founded Theranos in 2003, when she envisioned a device that could run comprehensive blood tests using only a few drops of blood. Holmes' vision was a breakthrough, and many people loved it.

Her charisma and vision attracted influential investors and board members, including former U.S. Secretaries of State George Shultz and Henry Kissinger. She raised over 700 million dollars without providing meaningful evidence that the technology worked, giving new meaning to "unicorn" startups with ballooning valuations.

By 2013, Theranos had secured significant partnerships with Walgreens and Safeway, promising to revolutionize blood testing in retail pharmacies. Holmes was everywhere, including the covers of magazines and speaking at prestigious events.

But inside Theranos, the story was very different. The Edison device was unreliable, producing inaccurate and inconsistent results.

The Decision Process

Holmes faced several critical decision points where she could have changed course. These points included:

Product Development Struggles. When it became clear that the Edison device wasn't working, Holmes could have paused commercialization to focus on solving the technical problems. Instead, she prioritized marketing over engineering. I have seen this in other tech startups on a different scale.

Investor Pressure. Holmes chose to manipulate data and stage product demonstrations rather than being transparent with investors about the company's challenges. Investor communications should be honest and accurate.

Regulatory Scrutiny. When regulators began questioning Theranos's practices, Holmes had the opportunity to come clean, but she chose not to.

The Results

Financial Collapse:

Theranos went from a high nine-billion-dollar valuation to zero and has proven to be a bust! I'd call this more than "learning." This is true failure, which is a word I do not like to use.

Destroyed Partnerships:

Holmes raked Walgreens and Safeway over the coals after they each invested in the partnership. Walgreens sued Theranos for 140 million dollars.

Legal Accountability:

Holmes was brought to justice in 2018 and was sentenced to prison for 11 years after her 2022 sentencing.

Patient results:

Patients who tried the device received inaccurate blood test results which led to more data showing that it did not work. These results could have been life or death for the patient.

How to Avoid This Mistake

There is a lot of history to unpack here. The Theranos story provides several important lessons for every CEO and entrepreneur.

Be Transparent:

Every startup faces setbacks. Investors, partners, and customers expect challenges, but will not tolerate lies and deception. Be truthful. Many startup founders tell stories that are incomplete until they have more testing and feedback. Learn to tell the truth, promising to fix known and identified shortcomings.

Prioritize Ethics Over Image:

Success at any cost is not real success. Ethical leadership means putting customers, employees, and public safety above personal ambition. It's about doing the right thing, even when it is difficult.

Validate Product Features and Benefits:

One lesson from the Theranos case is validating product specifications. The product or service might be excellent and offer much-needed benefits for customers, but it needs to be qualified and validated. No amount of aggressive marketing can compensate for a flawed product. Many of you may have similar experiences.

Encourage Open Communication:

CEOs should create a safe culture where anyone can discuss issues they see or experience without fear of retaliation. This is easier said than done. In the Holmes-created environment, everyone was held to secrecy, and no one could bring up issues they saw or experienced. True innovation thrives in open, collaborative environments.

Hire Experts and Listen to Them:

Surround yourself with complimentary people who have the expertise you lack. Holmes ignored scientific experts and pushed out dissenting voices, an approach that doomed Theranos, even though she pursued these experts.

Recovery and Moving Forward

For Holmes, recovery was impossible. The magnitude of her deception destroyed Theranos and her credibility. However, the tech industry has begun to learn from Theranos's mistakes. Investors demand more rigorous due diligence today, and healthcare startups face greater scrutiny to ensure safety and efficacy. We can expect some unique stories with AI now a critical part of our current and future healthcare.

Conclusion

Elizabeth Holmes set out to change the world, but her unwillingness to confront reality and her obsession with protecting her image led to one of the most spectacular business failures in history.

The key takeaway for CEOs?

Secret #24: Lead with integrity. Be open, honest, ethical, and accountable. There is no easy button. Execution matters. Trust matters. Truth Matters.

Holmes's downfall reminds us that your first responsibility as a CEO is to lead with integrity. There is a mini-series called, "The Dropout" that is dedicated to this story.

Chapter 25

Silence Is Complicity

A CMO did drugs with the sales team. Kevin Gaither knew. He stayed silent. And he regrets it to this day.

Kevin Gaither, now CEO of InsideSalesExpert.com, admits it was one of his biggest leadership failures and he will never forget it.

At a previous company, he found himself in a moment of truth, one that many executives encounter but few navigate well. As the SVP of Sales, he had built a high-performing team and was part of a rapidly growing company. But a single moment of hesitation when he chose silence over action became his self-admitted biggest leadership failure.

This is a story of inaction, of avoiding confrontation when the stakes were high, and of the lasting regret that follows when a leader fails to protect their team. It's also a story of learning, growth, and the commitment to never repeat the same mistake.

The Mistake

Kevin learned the hard way that failing to address serious misconduct head-on is just as damaging as committing the misconduct. His silence allowed the problem to grow, and the repercussions rippled far beyond what he could have predicted.

In a world where CEOs and senior leaders are responsible for culture, ethics, and accountability, Kevin's story serves as a warning to all CEOs and leaders: if you see something wrong and do nothing, you are part of the problem.

Setting the Stage: A Call That Changed Everything

At the time, Kevin was leading a strong sales team that he had built. The company was expanding, and morale was high. The leadership team, including the CMO, was well-respected and charismatic. There was no reason to question anyone's integrity, until the day a phone call shattered that assumption.

"Hey, KG, did you know the CMO took some of your salespeople onto the roof last night?"

At first, Kevin brushed it off. Maybe it was team bonding, so it was nothing unusual for a fast-moving, high-energy company.

Then came the next part:

"They were doing drugs up there."

Kevin's stomach dropped. He immediately knew this was a major problem. It was a scandal waiting to happen, a potential legal and reputational disaster.

And yet, instead of acting, he froze. Maybe you have experienced something similar, but this story should open your eyes!

The Decision Process: Fear vs. Leadership

Kevin's instinct told him exactly what needed to be done. But, instead of confronting the CMO or escalating the issue, he rationalized his inaction.

- Would speaking up make him look bad?
- Would it cause a political firestorm within the company?
- Would he be overreacting?
- Could this be a one-time lapse in judgment?

The CMO was well-liked and influential. Confronting him meant taking on a battle that could have consequences for Kevin's standing in the company. So, he chose silence.

In that moment, Kevin failed as a leader.

The Results: The Fallout of Avoidance

The consequences of inaction always catch up to you, and Kevin's mistake was no exception.

- He later found out this wasn't a one-time mistake. The CMO had a pattern of misconduct that went unchecked.

- By staying silent, he allowed toxic behavior to fester, damaging trust within the team.

- His credibility as a leader took a hit, his team saw the inaction, even if they never spoke about it directly.

- The company was put at risk, as this wasn't just an ethical issue. It was a legal liability waiting to explode.

And the worst part?

He carries that moment with him.

Kevin had a chance to protect his people. He didn't.

How to Avoid This Mistake

Kevin's story is not unique. Many leaders hesitate when faced with misconduct. But silence is never the right choice.

Here's is a **misconduct framework** for how CEOs and senior leaders can prevent this mistake:

- Act Immediately: The moment you become aware of misconduct, address it head-on. Delay only makes the problem worse.

- Gather the Facts: Document everything. If appropriate, take video if you can. Ask direct questions. Get clarity before taking your actions.

- Confront the Issue: Whether it's a peer, a direct report, or an executive, it's your job to hold them accountable.

- Escalate When Necessary: Don't let personal politics override the need to protect your team and company.

- Lead with Integrity: Your employees are watching. Your decision will set the tone for the entire culture.

Your silence is permission for bad behavior to continue. Don't let it.

Recovery and Moving Forward

Kevin learned from this mistake, but it still haunts him.

He couldn't undo the damage, but he made a commitment to himself: Never again would he hesitate in the face of misconduct.

Since then, he's made direct, immediate action a core part of his leadership philosophy. As I emphasize in my book, *The Rookie CEO, You Can't Make This Stuff Up!* - the CEO's philosophy is the foundation of their leadership.

Has the regret disappeared? No.

Has he become a stronger, better leader? Absolutely. He will never allow this again.

And, while the CMO was eventually removed, Kevin knows that his voice could have made it happen sooner, potentially preventing more damage along the way.

CEO Takeaways: What Every Leader Must Learn

- Ignoring misconduct makes you complicit.

- Fear and politics cannot override your duty to protect your team, company, and culture.

- Your credibility as a leader is on the line, because your team sees everything, and they are talking about it.

- Confronting the issue may be uncomfortable, but it's always necessary.

- If you stay silent, you're failing as a leader.

Conclusion

Leadership isn't just about hitting revenue targets or scaling a business. It's about doing what's right, especially when it's difficult.

Kevin's story shines this bright light: The hardest decisions define you as a leader.

Your company's culture is shaped by what you tolerate, as well as your leadership philosophy and style.

What kind of leader will you be? The one who looks the other way?

Or the one who stands up when it matters most?

The choice is yours. Don't flinch. Don't freeze. Do what's right. Every time. Because culture isn't what you say. It's what you allow. And silence screams.

Secret #25: Silence isn't neutral; it's permission. When you see something wrong and say nothing, you've made a choice. You've told your team what you're willing to tolerate.

Leadership means doing the uncomfortable thing when everyone else stays quiet. Your team watches how you handle tough moments. That's when trust is built or broken.

Don't flinch. Don't freeze. Do what's right. Every time.

Chapter 26

Integrity, Honesty, and Transparency

The Cyclone (from Chapter 8) was brilliant. Bold. And destined to fail. Why?

Because she traded speed for integrity and never recovered from the trust she lost.

She brought both consumer and large company formal training and background. A successful executive at her previous company, she brought all her philosophies to our company, and she was a very bright woman. While the Cyclone provided valuable learning experiences, the "what not to do" lessons proved to be more instructive.

There are two specific mistakes we are going to talk about in this chapter that poked huge holes in her CEO armor as it relates to leadership with integrity, honesty, and transparency.

We will expand upon the Cyclone's mistakes from *The Rookie CEO* book in the contour of this book for other CEOs to consider how to handle similar situations as they arise.

The Mistakes

There are two mistakes that created a wedge between her leadership team and building trust:

1. Open Conference Calls (when remote, especially)

2. Proprietary Information Management

Open Conference Calls

Many experts say that when you have received an offer for your new senior role, you should be deep into it on day one. The Cyclone took this seriously and was executing this concept with the senior leadership team (SLT). She had not relocated yet, but there were "staff meeting" calls weekly. As all leaders learned later, she had planned on bringing other executives to the company so she would bring previous loyalty with her rather than build it inside.

On the conference calls, she had invited those executives to join her in the same conference room to learn about everything they possibly could. We thought we were talking just to her, but we were talking to a small team of people (who all remained quiet) who would be coming with her in some capacity. One person would ultimately work for me, one would be a peer, and one would become my boss in a new senior level created above the current leadership team.

We learned about the Cyclone's loyalty to her current team over building loyalty with her new team, but it was not honest or transparent, and our team felt her integrity was in question from early on. Our leadership team was not impressed when we learned of her lack of transparency and questioned her integrity all along the way on every project, in every meeting, and on every call.

Proprietary Information

In early one on one meetings with senior leaders after she joined our company, the Cyclone distributed CDs (remember those?) marked "proprietary and confidential" to the team and asked us to replace their name with ours. This would become the new development process and company policy, impacting all projects, investments, business functions, and budgets. Seriously.

Setting the Stage

The Cyclone was a powerful CEO and wanted to show the new company and her new leadership team she was the boss. She set direction, tone, and priorities, and she made it very clear that we would do it her way.

She was uniquely different from the previous "Interim CEO," who was from a sales background. The Cyclone was passionate about installing her culture into a much older company with a broad international team of leaders and a totally different culture.

These two mistakes were specifically integrity-based. SLT members all had similar takes on her leadership style - that she was smart but an authoritarian leader. She surrounded herself with "yes" people.

The Decision Process

The Cyclone clearly wanted to make an impact as fast as possible. The "need for speed" drove her decision to let her loyal previous team in on her meetings when on remote conference calls. She wanted to change internally to her known development and business decision process from her previous company as fast as possible which drove her decision to have me edit the proprietary documents.

Her strategy aligned with an SHRM.org study that revealed 65% of CEOs regretted not moving faster in building their top teams and making the appropriate changes.

The Results

The Cyclone lost respect from most of the senior leadership team because of her need for speed versus integrity, honesty, and transparency. It made her new CEO role much harder than it should have which forced her to hire her trusted loyal team of the past to help her "tame the leadership culture" in her new company.

How to Avoid This Mistake

As a new CEO, the Cyclone entered a culture significantly different from her previous company. Both of her integrity missteps were avoidable and could have been addressed with straightforward, team-oriented actions. This **trust framework** will help guide you if your first CEO role is similar to the Cyclone's:

- Build Trust Through Transparency. Never invite external individuals, especially from your previous company to internal meetings without disclosing their presence. If they become employees, integrate them openly and ensure the existing team understands their roles and contributions. Transparency builds trust; secrecy destroys it.

- Collaborate on Process Improvement. Rather than imposing outside processes, leverage the knowledge and experience of your current team. Call a meeting with key leaders responsible for development and policies. Assign them to a "tiger team" tasked with assessing current processes, identifying what works and what doesn't, and aligning on improvements that support your vision. Under no circumstances should proprietary documents from a previous company be used; this compromises both legal standing and ethical integrity.

- Lead With Open Communications. Collaborate with your team, listening to feedback and understanding bottlenecks you can unblock.

- Review Overall Skill Sets of Your Team. Listen, learn, and be curious.

By taking these steps, the Cyclone could have quickly built trust, gained buy-in from her leadership team, and established a foundation for long-term success without compromising integrity, honesty, or transparency.

Recovery and Moving Forward

The consequences of the Cyclone's integrity missteps were far-reaching. Two senior executives chose to leave the company within a week of each other, landing at startups where trust and alignment with leadership were paramount. These departures signalled deeper issues within the organization, as trust in the Cyclone's leadership had rapidly eroded.

Five weeks later, after the departures, the Cyclone was removed from the CEO role. The parent company's appointed CEO stepped in to stabilize the situation, but the damage had already been done. Trust didn't just walk out with the departed executives. It collapsed internally, one departure at a time.

Once trust is broken, recovery is challenging, and it can be impossible without a complete overhaul of both leadership and culture.

Conclusion

Leadership isn't just about hitting goals. It's about *how* you get there. Integrity, honesty, and transparency aren't optional. They're the baseline for building real trust.

The Cyclone lost that trust early. She brought in people from her past without telling her new team. She reused proprietary documents from a previous company. From that moment on, her credibility was in question, and it never recovered. The result? Key leaders left. She was replaced. The division was eventually sold off.

Here's the truth: Trust is earned fast and lost just as fast. If your team doesn't trust how you operate, it won't matter how smart or strategic you are.

Respect people, the culture, and the rules. Lead with clarity. Be transparent. Stay grounded in the team you have, not just the one you used to trust.

Alignment comes from open dialogue and shared ownership, not from top-down orders. Build that, and you'll go far. Without integrity, even the brightest and most brilliant executives lose their edge. And their teams.

Secret #26: Trust is hard to earn and easy to lose. Decisions made without transparency and integrity can have long-lasting consequences that impact not only the organization's performance but also its people, reputation, and future viability.

Part 6

Team and Organizational Mistakes

Chapter 27

The High Cost of Delaying Change

Michael Williams knew he had to make changes. But he waited. The result? Lost partners. Declining sales. Eighteen months of growth destroyed.

This is what can happen when CEOs delay decisions they already know they need to make.

Michael Williams, president of a national service provider, learned that delaying difficult decisions can cause serious problems. In the fast-moving world of telecommunications, holding onto underperforming leadership can slow growth, damage partnerships, and set a company back by months, if not years.

Michael's story is a reminder of why CEOs need to trust both their instincts and the data and act decisively, even in the face of external pushback. One very critical success factor of top executives is to make rapid decisions with limited data, but you do need a personal decision process which becomes a habit to make the most informed decision possible as fast as possible.

I have known Michael for over 20 years, and we have worked in two companies together, albeit in different groups. He is the consummate professional executive, respected by his peers and subordinates. He brings a high level of empathy and compassion to his role.

The Mistake

Michael's mistake was waiting too long to replace a long-term C-level executive who was failing to drive sales growth. The warning signs were clear. Sales had dropped 40% year-over-year, and while the company was still growing, it was far from the projected expectations. The executive in charge of sales couldn't recruit effective sales performers and lacked a solid plan for recovery. Despite multiple conversations, setting clear expectations, and even hiring a sales operations manager to relieve the executive of non-sales tasks, there was no improvement. Top leaders were expected to handle performance issues rapidly.

When Michael decided to initiate formal disciplinary action, he faced resistance from the parent company's Human Resources (HR) VP who preferred to take a softer approach and give the executive more time. Against his better judgment, Michael agreed to delay formal action, a decision that would come at a significant cost.

Setting the Stage

Leading up to this mistake, the company was stalled. Sales growth had taken a sharp dive. The leadership team knew changes were needed, and Michael had engaged in multiple discussions with the sales executive to address the ongoing issues. Clear expectations were set, additional resources were provided, but the results were not improving.

Michael wanted to terminate the underperforming sales leader. But the parent company's HR leadership pushed back. He chose to comply with their wishes instead of following his instincts, which was backed by measurable data.

The Decision Process

Michael had already taken the steps to identify and address the problem. He recognized the underperformance, had honest conversations with the executive, and even brought in additional staff to clear non-sales-related tasks from the executive's plate. But when these efforts failed and he wanted to proceed with formal disciplinary action, the parent company overruled him, urging patience and more assistance.

Reluctantly, Michael agreed to their plan. But, deep down, he knew that more time wouldn't solve the core issue. This decision to delay action was made in the spirit of collaboration and out of respect for the parent company's input.

The Results

The decision to delay replacing the sales executive came with costs. Partners moved their business to other vendors reducing revenue even further.

Finally, the inevitable decision was made: The executive was finally exited from the company. But by that time, the damage was done. The delay had put the company's sales efforts behind schedule by an estimated eighteen months.

How to Avoid This Mistake

Hindsight can be both illuminating and painful. Michael now acknowledges that he should have trusted his instincts and pushed back against the parent company's decision. In his words, "I knew it. I just didn't act. And that cost us more than I ever imagined." When faced with critical leadership failures, it's essential for CEOs and leaders to advocate for the tough calls that would best serve the company's future.

Michael's learning lesson: don't wait. Trust your data backed instinct and judgment, especially when you've already assessed the situation and taken all reasonable steps to support improvement. Change is hard, but failing to act can be even more damaging.

Here is a simple **change leadership framework** to guide you and help you decide when to act:

- Is the leader causing active harm or stalling growth?

- Have you provided support and set clear expectations?

- If the answer is yes, it's time to act.

Recovery and Moving Forward

On Michael's recommendation, the sales team was merged into the parent company's sales management structure. This move brought new leadership and fresh momentum to the team. Within three months, sales began trending upward. By the six-month mark, sales goals were being exceeded.

What took eighteen months to damage took six months to rebuild.

Michael's open discussions with the parent company's chief operating officer (COO) revealed just how costly the delay had been. The realization that the company had lost about eighteen months of potential growth was sobering but reinforced the importance of making timely leadership changes.

Conclusion

Michael Williams' experience is a lesson that resonates with CEOs and business leaders at every level. The reluctance to make hard decisions can come from various pressures, whether from a parent company, investors, or even a desire to give people the benefit of the doubt. But when you know change is needed, delaying can cost your company time, revenue, and market credibility.

Secret #27: Don't postpone the inevitable. Trust your data backed instincts, make the difficult decision, and prevent greater problems from happening tomorrow.

Chapter 28

When Vision Blinds Leadership: Steve Jobs' Biggest Mistake at Apple

Visionary CEOs make mistakes. Steve Jobs is a great example.

Steve Jobs has been cited as one of the greatest visionaries in business history. His never-ending pursuit of perfection and innovation redefined multiple industries, from personal computing and animation to music and smartphones.

His leadership style got him fired from the company he founded and built. Why? Ego. Control. Blind Spots.

This story isn't about criticizing Jobs. It's about what every CEO must learn before it's too late.

The Mistake

Steve Jobs' greatest mistake was demonstrating his rough-shod style that essentially upset his team and the board of directors.

Leadership Style:

- Jobs was known for being abrasive and authoritarian. He led with a micro-management philosophy that tends to upset others.

Unrealistic Expectations:

- Jobs got involved in every aspect of product design, challenging his engineers to meet impossible deadlines, again upsetting his team members.

Internal Power Struggles:

- Jobs created a toxic work environment. Apple hired John Sculley as CEO, and Jobs then proceeded to interfere with Sculley's decision-making process at Apple.

Neglecting the Business Side:

- Jobs could not have cared less about any part of the business outside of products and their innovation.

These issues forced Jobs out of Apple in 1985, a devastating personal and professional experience. He was upset.

Setting the Stage

Steve Jobs and Steve Wozniak co-founded Apple Computer in 1976.

Their first product, the Apple I, took the market by storm, leading Apple to go public in 1980. IBM and Microsoft drove the highly competitive personal computer market.

They continued to innovate new products with mixed success. Jobs' focus became the Macintosh (Mac). However, Apple was now experiencing operations problems which drove Apple to hire John Sculley from PepsiCo. This new combination of people didn't work. They were in constant conflict. These powerful men hurt Apple's progress, and Jobs was fired.

The Decision Process: CEOs, Take Note

Leading up to Jobs' termination, it became clear he was interfering with everything Mac-related. He upset the team, his behavior was abrasive and super-intense, and he clashed with everyone, especially Sculley.

Here is the order of disorder:

- Sculley cut the Macintosh's marketing budget.

- Jobs tried to stage a coup to oust him.

- The board supported Sculley.

- Jobs resigned.

The Results

Once Steve Jobs left Apple, the visionary was gone!

Apple struggled. They had their operations expert in Sculley but had no GPS or rudder to steer the Apple ship. Apple's market presence and success declined.

- Jobs was a wounded warrior. As the founder and visionary of Apple, he felt like a failure because he was "Apple" to most people.

- After Jobs left, his early team followed him out of Apple's door, contributing to their lackluster company performance.

- Jobs realized he needed to work on his leadership capabilities in whatever he would do **NeXT** (pun intended).

How to Avoid This Mistake

Jobs' story offers timeless lessons for every CEO and leader:

- Vision matters when it aligns with the team

- Micro-management kills trust, innovation, and creativity.

- Hire the best A-players. Delegate to them, empower them, and trust them to execute their jobs.

- Manage your own ego and grow your emotional intelligence (EQ).

- Learn from setbacks and challenges and be fully self-aware.

- A strong team will eliminate your blind spots and make you a better leader.

Recovery and Moving Forward

Jobs founded **NeXT**, a new computer company that was a whirlwind, but its software became the foundation for Apple's future.

Jobs also purchased **Pixar** from George Lucas in 1986. Pixar led the evolving animation technology space and sold it for 7.4 billion dollars.

A few years later, Apple struggled to survive, so it acquired NeXT, bringing Jobs back. However, the next time around,

Jobs was a different leader. He had worked on his skills that he realized a few years earlier needed upgrading, and he returned with leadership maturity:

- He refined Apple's products.

- He was now a better collaborator.

- He focused on design and user experience.

- He delegated execution to operational leaders.

Jobs' return brought us the most successful products in history: the iMac, iPod, iPhone, and iPad, transforming Apple. He set up Apple to be the world's most valuable company.

Conclusion

Steve Jobs' greatest mistake was his leadership style. He had to leave Apple to find his future self, but this shows us that we can change, grow, and learn.

A quote from Steve that you may remember, is "Getting fired from Apple was the best thing that could have happened to me." – Steve Jobs, Stanford Commencement, 2005

Jobs' failures during his first stint at Apple made him the leader who would go on to change the world – with vision and wisdom.

Secret #28: Vision is powerful, but leadership sustains it and, in this case, changes the world!

Part 7

Startup Lessons - All Categories

Chapter 29

Cofounder's Dilemma

Think picking a cofounder is like picking a teammate? It's more like choosing a spouse. And if you get it wrong, the cost isn't just emotional; it's financial, legal, and personal.

Too many founders make this choice out of comfort, not clarity.

Finding the right cofounder is one of the most important decisions you will make for your startup. To many first-time founders, the decision is misunderstood because of the emotion and consequences attached to it. In the early-stage days, there is excitement and, often, the founder selects the cofounder because of friendship, relationship, technology knowledge, or some other influence. But the cofounder role brings with it the potential of many ways it can go sideways or badly for you.

Here is a simple **cofounder framework** for your potential engagement with cofounders:

- Align on mission, values, and vision before discussing what you will build and deliver.

- Clarify your roles, responsibilities, and decision rights for running the day-to-day business and towards outside investors, press, and customers.

- Discuss your financial goals, lifestyles, and targeted runway with full transparency. Does one of you need a market-based salary to survive? This is an unforeseen issue for some founders.

- Make it clear that you are the CEO, equity will not be split equally, and the CEO has the final decision if you reach an impasse.

- Create a founder agreement detailing everything possible with an experienced attorney, regardless of your relationship with the potential cofounder. This includes what happens if one of you leaves by choice or because of a disagreement.

The Mistake

The most common mistake? It is choosing a cofounder based on comfort or convenience, not common goals, not financial situation, or not alignment.

Some founders make the classic 50/50 equity split with their selected cofounder without ever being aligned with them on expectations, goals, or money. It can cost the founder everything.

Some founders select someone who wanted the title of cofounder but not the responsibility. Do not trust too quickly or skip the vetting, or you will pay the price.

Setting the Stage

Startups are hard. They are fast paced, with everything needing to be done and a lack of skills to do it all. Typically, first-time founders and even non-first-time founders do not have the skills to run the back office, human resources and policies, operations, sales, or marketing.

When you launch your company, the founders and first hires you surround yourself with will define your products, services, momentum, mindset, and culture.

In the early days, you think you need someone to share the load. You do, but not just anyone. There needs to be trust, confidence, and alignment between you on many items.

What you need is:

- Someone whose skills complement yours.

- A cofounder who shares the same goals and sense of urgency.

- Aligns on what "success" looks like in three, five, or ten years concerning the exit.

- Can handle stress and ambiguity, and pivots with maturity.

Do not make a mistake and skip the alignment of cofounders. If one prioritizes equity fairness, and the other prioritizes speed, it will likely not succeed. If neither prioritize compatibility, problems and disagreements will arise. Learn from these mistakes.

The Decision Process

There are key absolutes for you, the CEO. I assume your cofounder is not a co-CEO (which is not recommended) and will not have equal equity. Here are some guidelines for you, as CEO, for selecting your cofounder:

- Apply the framework above in your selection process.

- The CEO makes the final decision when you disagree. Only one person is the CEO and fully responsible.

- Do not split equity 50/50 or evenly across multiple founders.

- What happens if one of you wants out at any time?

- What happens if one of you wants the other cofounder out?

- Are you financially able to go without pay for six to twelve months? If not, what's the plan?

If you can't have that conversation up front, it's a red flag.

Sources like Harvard Business School professor Noam Wasserman ("The Founder's Dilemma," *Harvard Business Review*, 2008) show that 65% of high-potential startups fail due to cofounder conflict. The numbers may vary with different sources.

The Results

- One founder took on all the revenue generation while their selected cofounder drained cash. He had to borrow from the Small Business Administration (SBA) to buy him out.
- One founder lost control of her startup, took on IRS debt, and started over.

The wrong cofounder will cost you time, trust, capital, and your health.

How to Avoid This Mistake

Your process needs to analyze your cofounder choices and filter out red flags before you commit. Here is your list to execute this:

- Create a founder's agreement that articulates equity, expectations, decision rights, vesting, triggers, exit clauses and strategies, buyout clauses, and anything else that arises in discussions with advisors or legal counsel.

- Can we have uncomfortable discussions about money?

- Ensure core values are aligned. This is a must.

- Do we have complimentary and compatible skills?

- Jointly manage operations. Once started, hold weekly one on one alignment meetings, and discuss everything about the business.

Recovery and Moving Forward

Do you find yourself in a stressed cofounder relationship today? Be honest with yourself about the problem. Denial is a stage you may go through, but it drains your momentum. The road back from a bad cofounder decision can be very painful. Let's look at a compact **recovery framework** that I often recommend to CEOs and founders:

- Recognize: is the issue alignment? Goals? Roles? Values? Trust? Clarity?

- Restructure: Can it be repaired? What would this take?

- Rebuild: Recommit, build trust, create process with checkpoints.

Here's what to do:

- Meet with an arbiter to discuss what is, and is not, working.

- Decide if this partnership can be restructured and rebuilt or must it be ended.

- If you both think it can work, bring in the attorney to draft a founder agreement.

The two founders mentioned previously both rebounded and became stronger because they were willing to own the mistake, learn, and move forward with clarity. Their mistakes are specifically in the chapters that follow.

Conclusion

Startups are susceptible to founder fallout. It might not seem possible when you start, and it feels comfortable to have coffee or breakfast with someone else at the local coffee shop. It's like finding your life partner, though; it's not easy to find the right partner and the right alignment on goals, finances, and all the assets.

Choose wisely. Choose deliberately. Choose based on alignment, not emotion.

As one founder told me: "If I ever take on a cofounder again, we're going through business therapy first."

And another quote, "We didn't just survive our founder fallouts, we became better CEOs because of it."

Secret #29: A great cofounder multiplies your momentum. The wrong one multiplies your mistakes. Follow a process to vet and 100% align with your selected cofounder. Pick a cofounder like you're picking a spouse because, in some ways, it's harder to unwind.

Chapter 30

The High Price of Trust

Jody Gonzales, the founder and CEO of Viper Communications, made a mistake in 2017 that cost her nearly everything.

It's a story that many first-time CEOs can relate to and shows how a lack of patience, excitement for high-payoff potential, trust, and inexperience can impact your company.

Jody was all in. Determined to grow fast, she made a move that looked like a breakthrough, and it nearly broke the company. That decision ultimately led to the collapse of her first startup. But from the wreckage, she took the lessons, regrouped, and went on to build a thriving second venture.

The Mistake

In 2017, Jody's company took on a project that seemed like a quick win to propel the business to new heights. Viper Communications started expanding into low-voltage and security installations for small businesses. A salesperson brought in a promising project to subcontract fiber-to-the-home (FTTH) work for Altice, a primary regional telecom provider, before being acquired by Cablevision. The project involved running fiber over existing coax cables in New Jersey and New York. They would be paid by the foot, and with millions of feet of cable to be laid, it appeared to be a vast, lucrative opportunity to propel Viper Communications.

Jody rented bucket trucks, hired linemen, and put the company into full swing. However, there was one crucial problem: no formal contract. After months of expensive labor and equipment rentals, the Chicago-based contractor who hired them vanished, leaving Jody's company out more than $200,000. Then Altice brought the project in-house, leaving Jody unpaid, exposed, and with no legal recourse.

Setting the Stage

Jody trusted the salesperson who brought in the deal, despite having no previous relationship with the contractor. There was no written agreement, no milestones or deliverables, and no clearly defined expectations on either side.

Jody had little experience with these kinds of projects. She saw a significant opportunity that brought her overwhelming excitement for potential revenue and profit. Based on that, she made a decision that would later bring on catastrophic consequences.

The Decision Process

Jody's decision was driven by excitement and ambition. She saw dollar signs and potential growth and assumed that the project would succeed simply because of the scale.

However, the pressure for a startup to grow and be successful can sometimes cloud your judgment as the founder and CEO. Jody overlooked basic business processes, which included:

- The lack of a formal services contract.

- Statement of work with defined deliverables and milestones.

- A backup plan.

The Results

The impact of this mistake was devastating. Jody went an entire year without paying herself and nearly lost her home. The company struggled so Jody made the difficult decision to leave Viper Communications to find a stable job. Her shady business partner, whom she later discovered had failed to pay payroll taxes for over a year, continued to run the business into the ground. The IRS opened an investigation, and Jody was left to clean up the mess, owing six figures in back taxes.

This was a low moment for Jody. She had shown integrity and commitment to her clients. Former clients and resellers reached out, sharing feedback. They wanted to work with her, not her partner.

They were eager to work with Jody, and this presented her with an unexpected new opportunity.

How to Avoid This Mistake

Jody now tells founders: Be honest about what you know how to deliver, and don't ignore the early warning signs when something doesn't add up. The salesperson who brought in the deal had a sketchy reputation. She didn't vet it fully. She didn't press for details. That silence became expensive.

The bigger mistake? Moving forward without a written agreement. No contract. No timeline. No payment structure. No written expectations. She also never developed a backup strategy. When the deal unraveled, she was exposed.

Recovery and Moving Forward

Jody walked away from Viper with nothing but her reputation intact. It took time to clear her head. She had no answers, no easy path. But then, her former customers reached out to ask for her help and support. They were dissatisfied with the way things were being run. That told her something. There was still trust and demand. So, she built something new: Axtel Consulting. No marketing push. Just results. And those clients? They came with her.

This was Jody's recovery! Axtel Consulting thrived, and Jody's reputation for delivering results and supporting her clients helped her build a new business. She was able to strike a deal with the IRS over the payroll taxes, although she never thoroughly learned what happened to her former partner, who later went on to receive millions in funding for a new venture.

Let's put Jody's recovery into Chapter 29's Framework of Recognize – Restructure – Rebuild:

Jody's Turnaround: What It Really Took

1. Recognize

The project failed. The money was gone. Her partner bailed. Jody didn't sugarcoat it.

- She admitted she ignored warning signs.

- She saw where trust replaced due diligence.

- She took full responsibility and made the decision to stop digging.

You can't fix the business until you face the facts.

2. Restructure

She couldn't patch Viper back together. But she could take control of what came next.

- She shut it down and dealt with the fallout.

- She squared up with the IRS.

- She stayed in touch with the clients who still backed her.

Walking away wasn't quitting, it was clearing space to start fresh.

3. Rebuild

When the time was right, she launched again, but this time, on her terms.

- Contracts came first. So did accountability.

- Her new company, Axtel Consulting, started lean and grew fast.

- Clients returned, not because she asked, but because they trusted her.

Jody didn't bounce back. She built back stronger and smarter.

Conclusion

Jody Gonzales' story raises awareness for first-time CEOs who need to understand the dangers of trusting too easily, rushing into business without proper safeguards, and allowing excitement to override strong business principles and best practices. But it's also a story of resilience. Jody learned from her mistake, rebuilt her career, and today, runs a successful consulting firm.

There is a clear lesson here. Always vet new opportunities thoroughly, ensure you have contracts in place, and never let excitement be a blind spot for you by creating potential risks. Most importantly, have a backup plan for when things don't go as expected. Because, as Jody's story shows, the cost of not doing so can be far greater than you might think.

Secret #30: Trust is earned. Verification is required. Startup CEOs must protect their company with contracts, controls, and clear decision rights, because one misstep can cost everything they've built. Remember this when selecting a cofounder.

Chapter 31

When Cofounders Turn Toxic

Bill McClain's eagerness to start his first company led to cofounder blind spots he was unaware of or prepared for.

Bill McClain, the founder and CEO of Network Solutions, met his initial cofounder in an IT firm before he started his first company. His field partner and subject matter expert wanted to be a business owner, and together, they decided to cofound Networking Solutions. They had built a relationship after both were shortchanged by their larger employer which had promised equity, but it never came. They formed the company with a 50/50 ownership structure.

This 50/50 partnership was Bill's mistake that cost him time, money, and patience. This is a story that many cofounders can relate to, and here is why. They never discussed expectations, personal financial situation, goals, and strategies.

The Mistake

In 1996, Bill and his cofounder were well-positioned in the market transition period, moving from older coax and twisted pair telecom networks to Ethernet and IP networks, which is what Networking Solutions was providing to their customers. Bill is proud that they never missed a payroll, even in difficult times and partner disagreements.

The 50/50 partner structure proved to be a mismatch, because the two cofounders never discussed demands on their time, priorities, financial situations, work ethics, and their overall styles, which all led to a communications debacle. Bill described it much like a bad marriage, and there were many lessons learned.

Simply put, there was a complete mismatch of each cofounder's modus operandi.

Setting the Stage

The company was able to start with previous customers from the larger organization they both left. They had a shoestring budget, but with their sweat equity, as in many bootstrapped startups, they were able to get going with minimal resources.

They had an accounting firm partner, rented an office, and bought personal computers, office equipment, and a phone system for all employees. They felt all set to go and grow their new business.

The Decision Process

Due to their road warrior experience together at the larger company, Bill and his partner were initially comfortable with each other, so they settled on the 50/50 equity structure. Seems like a simple decision, but they left out key discussion points beyond equity. This included financial expectations and ongoing needs. For example, how bonus payments would be managed and the use of cash vs. reinvestment in the company. These are major decision processes on company direction, policies, and debt.

Bill's wife was a CPA, but his partner lacked financial security and insisted on taking more cash out of the business to pay himself. This was a significant economic disconnect.

His cofounder wanted to take bonus cash from jobs, while Bill wanted to reinvest in the business to fuel future growth with this cash. They added an administrative assistant and an inside sales cold-calling resource to the company in the 1997-98 timeframe and had to finance these salaries.

By 1998 or 1999, Bill realized his cofounder was no longer motivated or happy with his money situation. But Bill was delivering 85% of the revenue, and the company was in debt.

In 1999, the two cofounders had a meeting to restructure, which required either a buyout or shutdown. Bill went to the Small Business Administration (SBA) to apply for a loan to help him buy out his cofounder.

The Results

The impact of this mistake was that Bill could have executed more quickly and successfully without a partner. It took seven years to pay back the SBA assistance to dig out of debt.

How to Avoid This Mistake

This was described by Bill as simply, "Do not get a partner cofounder. Do it yourself!" He feels he could have created, built, and grown the business more easily without a cofounder. He would have had far fewer headaches and risks. As it was, he almost lost his company! This may not apply to all cofounders, but in Bill's case, it was a reality.

Recovery and Moving Forward

Bill McClain didn't just survive the fallout. He turned the mistake into momentum. Post buyout, it took years to recover. Bill started StratusDial, another startup that was complementary to Networking Solutions, in 2011. This was a huge move forward, as StratusDial generated recurring revenues. This was a monumental move forward in Bill's recovery. He now had two companies: Networking Solutions and StratusDial. Joint solutions are widespread today between the two companies. Bill has now started a third company, and there are more details in the Bonus Section that follows.

Let's put Bill's recovery into Chapter 29's Framework:

1. Recognize

Bill realized what was broken:

- A cofounder without shared financial priorities.

- A deadlocked 50/50 structure that was unable to be resolved.

- The company lost momentum

This was not going to work.

2. Restructure

He met with his cofounder. Together, they made the decision: buyout or shutdown.

- Bill pursued an SBA loan.

- He bought out the cofounder.

- He assumed full control, responsibility, and the burden of debt.

The move was painful but necessary.

3. Rebuild

Bill didn't stop. He doubled down:

- He stabilized Networking Solutions.

- He launched a second company, StratusDial, focused on recurring revenue.

- Eventually, he co-founded UponAI with Jody Gonzales, but only after deep alignment.

He built a stronger business ecosystem, learned from the past, and now leads with clarity and control.

Conclusion

Selecting the wrong cofounder is one of the most common mistakes made by founders.

When you embark on finding and selecting cofounders, make sure:

- You have common goals.

- You understand their financial situation and cash demands.

- You structure equity where you, the CEO, are the primary founder and always maintain control.

- Vet your cofounder candidates.

For first-time founder CEOs, Bill's experience offers a clear lesson: Always think through whether a cofounder is necessary to be successful. If so, structure equity appropriately, and create bylaws and a business model that allow you to always maintain control.

Bonus Section

Despite this mistake, and that of Jody Gonzales, also featured in this book with a similar cofounder mistake, Bill McClain and Jody Gonzales have teamed up to cofound a third company for each of them called UponAI. In my interviews with them both, they provided me with the reasons why they have both taken on a cofounder together. Both cofounders have:

1. The exact financial expectations and goals: alignment.

2. The same financial demands: alignment and goals.

3. Unparalleled work ethics: alignment.

4. Overlapping philosophies: alignment.

5. They have both experienced cofounder "divorces": experiences aligned.

They both are CEOs of two other companies already. For UponAI, both are managing directors, and Bill is CEO, and Jody is CTO. As of the writing of this book, UponAI is hot and signing up new customers on an ongoing basis.

Secret #31: Never split 50/50 with your cofounder. You are the CEO. Own the role, set the direction, and structure equity so that control and decision rights remain clear and undisputed.

Chapter 32

The Negotiation Muscle Every CEO Must Build

Negotiate or lose millions of dollars!

Robert, a first-time founder and CEO, didn't realize that the most essential skill he needed wasn't technical or visionary. It was negotiation. And, like many startup CEOs, he didn't know he needed it until it was too late.

Every inflection point in a CEO's journey is a negotiation, from funding to hiring, from board management to exits. And the earlier you build this skill, the fewer regrets you'll carry forward.

The Mistake: Thinking Negotiation Is Just About Deals

Robert's early mistakes weren't made at the negotiating table. They happened before he knew he was negotiating, like when he chose his cofounder. Or when he handed out equal equity shares to feel "fair" and get "buy-in" from his cofounders. Or when he assumed an investor's term sheet was nonnegotiable.

It all started when he raised his first round. The investor liked his vision but demanded 51% of the company in exchange. Robert, who needed the money and lacked options, agreed. Along with the majority ownership came board control and, eventually, maybe a new CEO.

Robert learned the fine print through both the investors and the founders' lenses. He negotiated from a place of need, not strength, and assumed that being CEO in title meant being in charge.

Setting the Stage

Negotiation isn't just a skill. It's your armor. Your leverage. Your ability to protect the company, your team, and your vision.

These are some of the things that startup CEOs negotiate every day:

- Selecting cofounders
- Allocating equity

- Hiring A-players

- Setting salary plus equity packages

- Structuring term sheets for investments

- Managing the board of directors

- Locating ideal partnerships to scale the business

- Negotiating your role in the company's future

- Negotiate project schedules

- And more, depending on the type of company, structure, and money model

The problem? Most founders treat these like conversations, not negotiations. Robert did, too.

The Decision Process

Robert was negotiating at the time, but not necessarily from a position of strength:

- Giving up 51%+ isn't just about equity; it's also about control. He did his best under the conditions.

- Equal equity among cofounders with unequal contributions, which he did to gain team buy-in and confidence, turned out to be a disaster and was challenging to manage.

- There are different types of investors, many who haven't built companies, especially in your market. They could struggle to understand your business and your decision-making process.

He learned that every time you say "yes" to a term, a role, or a deal, you're either preserving your ability to lead or handing it over.

Do your best to get these answers, and be curious about anything your mind questions:

- What happens if my investor wants me out?

- What protections do I need, or should I try to secure, in the term sheet?

- How will this equity split hold up in three years? Five years? At exit?

He just signed and paid the price.

The Results

Robert lost control of his board. He struggled to remove a toxic CTO who held equal equity. He couldn't hire the head of sales he needed, because he'd already given away too much equity. He had the title of CEO but lacked the power to lead. He did the best he could.

And yet, he wasn't the only one. This happens all the time. Sometimes, founders negotiate themselves into corners they can't escape from because they have limited choices at the time.

How to Avoid This Mistake

Master the art of negotiation early. It's not about being slick; it's about being prepared. You might consider reading *Never Split the Difference* by Chris Voss. This is an outstanding resource to master negotiation.

Start with your cofounder.

- Choose someone who complements you, not duplicates you.
- Set clear roles, equity splits based on contribution and risk, and vesting schedules.

Structure equity intentionally.

- The CEO must hold enough equity to make strategic calls and lead.
- Include standard four-year vesting with a one-year cliff for all founders.

Know your deal terms cold.

- Negotiate board seats, protective provisions, and decision rights.

- Use experienced legal counsel, as this is not where you save money.

Treat investors like coleaders, not overlords.

- Seek professional investors who have succeeded (or failed) *in your market.*

- Ask tough questions. If they get defensive, walk away.

Negotiate with the long game in mind.

- Alignment with the exit strategy is key.

- Save equity in a pool of shares for future hires and follow-on funding.

Get comfortable with hard conversations.

- Whether hiring, firing, fundraising, or aligning on direction, these are negotiations. Own them.

Recovery and Moving Forward

It wasn't a clean fix. Negotiating his way back into control meant legal wrangling, tense board meetings, and challenging conversations with his remaining team. But he learned to lead from leverage, not hope.

Robert eventually renegotiated his board structure and bought out a cofounder. But it took years and was messy.

Now, Robert's advice to founders includes:

- Be generous, but never naive.

- Be collaborative.

- Be trusting, but cautious.

But, above all, remember that if you don't negotiate for what you need, you will lose out in the future when it matters most.

Conclusion

Negotiation isn't an event. It's a daily discipline.

Founders who negotiate well don't just raise better funding rounds at the best available terms at the time or build stronger teams. They also create the conditions for sustainable leadership and company growth.

The best negotiators don't just win terms. They preserve the right to lead.

Secret #32: You negotiate more than you think: equity splits, investor terms, and your title. Every "yes" or "no" either gives you power or gives it away. If you're not negotiating, you're being negotiated. CEOs lead with leverage, not just vision.

Chapter 33

The Cost of Trust Without Verification

You hire the best legal experienced assistance. You trust them. They fail you. Now what?

The Architectologist, founder and CEO of a Florida-based late-stage startup, learned all about how first-time founders navigate new roadmaps and are offered advice from every angle. The mistake wasn't just trusting the wrong person. It was not verifying a legal task tied to ownership and was taking too long to resolve.

The Vision

A Florida startup had one goal: build durable, rapid-deploy housing for areas hit by hurricanes. What started as a simple disaster relief solution grew into something bigger, a modular weather-resistant housing system that could evolve into permanent homes, wired with smart tech. The mission was bold: rethink how the world builds modular weather resistant affordable homes which could be built and move-in ready in days not months.

The founder, known as the Architectologist, built a small local team and started building. Money was tight. Time was tighter. But they kept pushing.

The Mistake

The Architectologist's biggest mistake was putting too much trust in the wrong person. His investor-advisor, who also wore the CTO hat, was responsible for executing a stock repurchase agreement with a terminated employee. It should've been a routine task. His outsourced legal counsel and the CTO did not follow their own process to ensure the tasks were completed per the equity agreement.

Instead, it got botched. The advisor failed to follow through and didn't execute it properly or on time. The result? The unvested shares stayed with the ex-employee and outside the founder's control. This remained a problem for years.

As a first-time founder, the Architectologist had his hands full. He was doing everything, including running operations, raising capital, building the product, and managing personal stress on top of it all.

He assumed the legal advisor had it handled. He didn't double-check. That's where it broke down. You, as the founder CEO, are accountable for it all!

Then it got worse. The person he brought in to help clean up the mess, as it turned out, was secretly working with the terminated employee. That kind of betrayal cuts deep and added another layer of legal and ethical headaches that have taken several years to resolve.

This was a hard-earned lesson: When it comes to your capitalization table (cap) and critical business and legal agreements, trust isn't enough. You need proof.

The Results

This hit hard. It drained the Architectologist and his team financially and emotionally. Morale took a dive, and the cap table stayed a mess. Even though he had every legal right to fix it, the Architectologist didn't have the time, money, or energy to fight that battle while also trying to build a company.

And the problem didn't just sit there. It also blocked growth. The unresolved shares created too much noise for potential investors. They liked the product, and the vision, but the cap table gave them pause. That kind of uncertainty can be a deal killer.

What looked like a small misstep turned into a long-term drag on the company. It's a reminder that, when you're a founder, the details matter, especially the ones tied to ownership and control. It gets more difficult when early employees leave the company and they have equity options.

How to Avoid This Mistake

If you're a first-time founder, take this one to heart: Due diligence is not optional. It's your responsibility to get every detail right. When it comes to your capitalization table and legal agreements, hire a competent attorney, one who knows startups and understands founder risk. Get everything in writing, track dates, and follow up. Don't assume it's managed properly unless you've verified it yourself.

And here's a small but critical habit: Send anything legal via certified mail with a signature required. You'll be glad you did if things ever go sideways.

The other big takeaway? Don't drag your feet when someone on your team isn't working out. Fire fast. Waiting only creates more issues, culturally, legally, and emotionally. You're not just protecting the company. You're protecting your sanity.

Here is a **CAP table checklist** for first-time CEOs and founders:

- Terminated employees typically still hold unvested shares.

- No paper trail for buybacks or transfers?

- No audit of equity agreements every 6 months?

- Are verbal commitments documented?

- Are outsiders managing your share ledger?

- When did you last review and update the CAP table and shareholder agreements with your attorneys?

Recovery and Moving Forward

Despite the setback, the Architectologist has managed to keep the startup moving forward. At the time of the mistake, the company was still in the research and development phase, which limited the immediate impact on the business. He didn't get that time back. But what he gained was sharper judgment, legal precision, and a sixth sense for sketchy advisors. The startup survived. More importantly, so did he.

For first-time CEOs, this story is an eye-opening wake-up call. Clean up your cap table early. Stick to the agreements. Use an attorney who knows startups. Track every step. If you let the small stuff slide, it becomes big stuff fast and it can block your future.

Conclusion

The Architectologist's story is a real-life example of what happens when trust takes the place of verification. You can lean on your team, but you can't hand off accountability.

If the paperwork involves ownership or equity, check it yourself. Investors and your board will. If you don't, you'll be the one cleaning up the mess.

For founders, especially those in the early stages, the rules are clear:

- Sweat the details.

- Build your trusted team

And here's the good news: A mistake doesn't mean the end. If you stay sharp, own what went wrong, and course-correct fast, you can still build the business you imagined from the start.

Secret #33: As a startup CEO, you own the capitalization table and all legal and financial agreements of the company. Even if you delegate, you are accountable. Verify every contract, capitalization table, option grant, and termination personally. Manage your capitalization table like your company depends on it, because it does! If it's messy, your business will be, too. Know every line, every share, and every agreement, because your investors will. Details matter!

Chapter 34

Too-Good-to-Be-True Partnership

After two costly cofounder disasters, Jody Gonzales and Bill McClain made themselves a promise: never again. Both had lost time, money, and momentum by choosing the wrong partners in the past. They swore that if they ever joined forces with someone again, it would only be with complete alignment.

Today, they're proving that promise can pay off.

Their newest venture, **UponAI**, adds AI Agent capabilities to business phone systems, handling customer calls, sales calls, and everyday productivity tasks around the clock. The company is growing faster than any of Bill's or Jody's other businesses, but the real story is the foundation underneath it: trust, clarity, and shared values.

Jody and Bill didn't just jump in. They compared goals. They matched financial expectations. They divided roles and responsibilities with precision. Every decision was intentional. It's the opposite of how they started their earlier ventures, and it shows.

For startup founders, picking a cofounder is one of the most consequential choices you'll ever make. The same is true when selecting any business partner. Poor alignment on values, money, or decision-making will sink a good idea before it ever has a chance to grow.

Cofounder and Business Partner Alignment Checklist

Ask these questions when selecting your cofounder or business partner:

- Do their skills and decision style complement yours?

- Do they share your core values?

- Are financial expectations in sync?

- Have you agreed on equity, decision rights, and responsibilities?

- Will they negotiate openly and fairly?

- What does your gut say?

- What does the data say? Look at history, track record, and references.

- Have you discussed exits, "what if" scenarios, and contingencies?

- Are your roles and long-term vision clear?

- Would you be proud to introduce them to investors, customers, and employees?

The wrong answer to even one of these can create cracks you'll regret later.

Conclusion

Selecting a cofounder for your startup seems a straightforward part of your initial plans. It is possible to find the right partner, but it must be done with a vision, mission, and with a well-thought-out plan. If you follow the frameworks and guidelines covered in this section, you will increase your success rate by a 10X factor. The cofounder and business partner checklist and the secret provided here are your path to your successful startup

Secret #34: Great partnerships don't happen by accident. Do the work. Ask the hard questions. Only move forward when values, vision, and trust are fully aligned, because getting it wrong can cost you everything.

Part 8
Wrap Up

Chapter 35

The Importance of Continuous Learning and Reflection

You are too busy to be self-aware, to build new habits to improve day-to-day operations, and can't figure out how to get your head above water. You lose sleep. Think about every little thing in the shower. Can you "fix" those nuances that steal your brain cycles?

Not a good idea to run your company and daily life this way.

Every CEO starts somewhere, and the path they take shapes how they lead. In my first book, *The Rookie CEO, You Can't Make This Stuff Up!* I shared that each leader builds their foundation over time. For the best CEOs, that foundation is created and built with continuous learning. They gain knowledge from books, from peers, from the job itself, and from the hard lessons only experience can teach.

Are their philosophies filled with always-on learning? If so, are they learning from books? Classes? On-the-job training? The CEO's approach to this topic is their education. The best and most successful CEOs are continuous learners themselves and implement some form of learning from their experiences and their company.

This chapter isn't about humility, for humility's sake. It's about survival, growth, and transformation. Because if you don't evolve faster than your company, your company will outgrow you. It happens quietly, at first. Then it happens all at once. Boom! Your CEO role is lost. Don't let that happen! It's in your hands. Act now to reinforce tour future.

You're Either Learning, or You're Losing

If you picked up this book, you're in one of three places.

- You may be leading for the first-time and feel the heavy weight on your shoulders every day.

- Maybe you've plateaued and can't identify why or can't figure out how to break out.

- You may be pursuing a CEO role and want to avoid the landmines others have stepped on.

Good. That's where authentic leadership begins and when curiosity overrides ego.

I've learned this by coaching many CEOs, interviewing operators, and standing beside first-timers in the trenches: The best CEOs treat learning as a leadership discipline. It's not a phase; it's not a book-a-year ritual. It's how CEOs operate, reflect, and recover.

And yes, how they win!

Mistakes Are the Curriculum

Let me be clear: Every CEO in this book made mistakes. Many of them were costly, and some of them were catastrophic.

The Dealmaker pushed a risky deal to the cofounders. The Cyclone buried her team under a storm of cleverness. The General waited so long to act that his team almost gave up. Different leaders, same outcome, and each paid for the lesson, and each emerged sharper.

But here's the thing. All these CEOs *learned*. Sometimes slowly. Often painfully. But they came out the other side sharper, more self-aware, and more equipped.

Mistakes aren't the end. They're the tuition.

The CEO Day-to-Day Operating System: Curiosity Plus Courage

At the center of every strong CEO's mindset is a constant loop powered by two forces that keep the business moving forward: curiosity and courage.

Curiosity is that itch you can't ignore. It's the driving need to find out what you don't yet know. It's the question in the back of your mind: *How does this part of the business work? Where are the weak spots? What am I not seeing?*

It makes you dig in. You ask more questions and listen longer. You catch the angles others miss.

But curiosity alone is nothing more than a pile of notes. Courage is what makes you act on what you've learned, even when it's uncomfortable. It's changing direction because the facts demand it. It's grooming your replacement because the business needs a different leader. It's letting someone go when it must be done, even if it hurts. It's standing in front of your team to admit a mistake, apologizing without excuses, and making it right.

Put curiosity and courage together, and you do more than improve your skills. You build trust. You sharpen your instincts. You become the leader top talent wants to follow.

Reflection Is a Ritual, Not a Reaction

You don't need a crisis to reflect. Innovative CEOs build reflection into their weekly rhythm. Try creating a "weekly mirror" meeting. I've kept a Friday "mirror meeting" for years. I consider it part of my "administration Friday" on an ongoing basis.

I open my calendar and ask myself hard questions: Did I lead the things that matter? Who needed to hear from me and didn't? What decision am I still avoiding? The mirror never lies. Write it down. Say it out loud. Sit with it. Talk it through with your coach, advisor, or peer group. And then decide: What do I want to do differently next week?

This is the hidden power move: Reflection creates the conditions for rapid growth without the trauma of repeated failure.

The Best CEOs Aren't the Smartest. They're the Fastest Learners.

Let that sink in. In nearly every company I've worked with or advised, the most effective CEOs weren't the ones with the most credentials or charisma. They were the ones who learned the fastest.

Learning is a lifelong superpower that compounds over time for everyone, not just CEOs.

You Don't Have to Do This Alone

You hear this many times from different sources, even many CEOs: The CEO role is lonely, but it doesn't have to be isolating. How do you solve this loneliness issue?

Leverage available resources:

- Coaches who challenge your thinking.

- Advisors who've seen what you haven't.

- Peers who hold you accountable.

- Mentors who've made the mistakes before you.

- A top-notch leadership team of A-players who are open and honest with you.

Everyone you work with, for, and around will thank you for being self-aware.

Conclusion

There are many factors in your success in being a CEO. Being CEO isn't about being the smartest person in the room. It's about being the one who learns the fastest, the one who learns to leverage resources to help you shine and push through challenges, the one who reflects and acts. That edge comes from curiosity you practice daily and reflection you refuse to skip.

Don't wait for a crisis to force growth. Build learning into your operating system. Make reflection a ritual and act when necessary. Stay curious, stay courageous, and stay self-aware.

Secret #35: The best CEOs aren't the smartest in the room, they're the ones who learn the fastest, reflect continuously, and act rapidly when it's necessary. These are the critical success factors to stay ahead of your company's growth curve and the reason your team will believe in you and your confidence.

TOP SECRET

Chapter 36

Confidence Is Power

Confidence is a CEO's secret advantage. Without it, decisions stall, teams lose faith, and the business drifts. With it, you can lead in chaos, take hits, and still move forward.

Confidence isn't ego or bravado. It's not blind optimism, either. It's knowing yourself. It's knowing what you stand for. And it's making the tough calls when the pressure's on and the room gets tense, and you stay calm.

First-time CEOs often confuse confidence with certainty. They wait for the perfect plan, the perfect moment, or the perfect hire before acting. But seasoned CEOs know that confidence is built on motion. It's the byproduct of decisions, lessons learned, mistakes recovered from, and trust earned, first in yourself and then in others.

Before we get to the list of what confidence allows you to do, here's a real story of what confidence looks like in action.

One CEO I worked with was facing a brutal board meeting after missing the quarter. Revenue was down, forecasts were shaky, and the board was ready to pounce. The boardroom was quiet, but the tension was in the air. Everyone knew the numbers were bad. He walked in with calm, not excuses. He displayed confidence in himself. The first slide went up as he delivered with no fluff and no spin. He anticipated the top fifty questions he might be asked and built backup slides for each one.

The board, expecting excuses, got clarity. They expected defensiveness but got transparency. His preparation, poise, and authenticity changed the entire room. They walked out saying, "He's got this." That's what real CEO confidence looks like.

Confidence is what allows you to:

- Step into a boardroom where everyone's done this fifty times before and still own it.

- Hire someone better than you and not feel threatened.

- Fire someone when it's the right decision, even when it hurts.

- Say "I don't know" without losing respect.

- Let go of the deck, the feature, or the deal because you trust your team.

- Show up, day after day, through setbacks, silence, and sprints.

Confidence isn't given. It's built. And the best CEOs build it brick by brick. They are self-aware.

- They reflect weekly using rituals or habits.

- They ask for help when it's clear they need it.

- They hire coaches and advisors because they don't need to do everything alone.

- They learn from their mistakes instead of hiding from them.

- They don't chase perfection; they pursue progress.

Powerful leadership is magnetic. People follow a confident CEO not because of their title, but because of how they show up. How they lead in uncertainty. How they protect the mission. How they care for the team.

And here's the truth: You already have what it takes. You don't need a new title or new funding to lead with confidence and power. You must commit to showing up, keep learning, and keeping sharp every day!

Conclusion

Confidence is your edge. Power is your presence. Use them.

Confidence is a built and earned discipline. It's built in the boardroom, in the tough calls, and in the quiet moments of reflection when no one is watching. It's earned by moving forward, learning fast, and owning every outcome.

That's where real confidence comes from. Momentum, resilience, and truth.

Secret #36: Confidence isn't luck. It's earned in the daily grind and in every hard call, every missed shot you own, every lesson you don't dodge. Stack those wins, own those losses, and you'll carry a presence no title can give you. That's the power people follow.

Chapter 37

Recap of All Secrets

Secret #1: Pay attention to the people who care about you. Step away when you need to. Balance isn't a luxury; it's how you stay in the game. Revenue may rise and fall, but the time, laughter, and love you share with family and friends are the things that truly last.

Secret #2: As founder, first-time CEO, or serial CEO, you need a number two. It might be a cofounder, an outside coach, or a senior executive leader on your team. The title does not matter. The trust does!

Secret #3: If your only plan must work, it probably won't. The CEOs who survive are the ones who build options early so they can pivot fast and zig when the market zags.

Secret #4: Be self-aware and fully market-aware of your surroundings in the marketplace. It will prevent blind spots and help you manage dishonest competitors.

Secret #5: Don't let pride and ego cloud your judgment! The cost is high. This may be hard to do, because most CEOs have a higher level of pride, especially in their company. Hint: Ego feels like strength, but it's a trap. Pride can sink your company faster than a bad idea. Know when to lead with principle and when to let it go!

Secret #6: Innovation is not a threat; delaying adoption and investment is. Watch for innovation and change relentlessly. Map your strengths, weaknesses, opportunities, and threats (SWOT). Your leadership team and subject matter experts should be actively involved in keeping you abreast with market dynamics and threats and maintain an ongoing SWOT analysis. Hint: A CEO who stops listening and learning becomes the company's biggest risk.

Secret #7: The deal is not done when it is signed. Integration leverages where value is created or destroyed. Integration requires planning, leadership, and discipline exactly as the acquisition itself does. If you're not personally driving the integration as the CEO, then someone else is, and it might not be in the direction you had envisioned.

Thus, keep in mind who you would trust to lead an acquisition, should it happen. Write a draft plan. Identify areas of weakness where you need help to shut down blind spots.

Secret #8: Clarity is your superpower. Confusion kills culture. Keep it simple. Set clear expectations early. Confirm understanding consistently.

Secret #9: Hire great people and set clear expectations and goals. Trust them to deliver. Micromanagement is a culture killer. Replace it with autonomy, support, curiosity, and accountability.

Secret #10: Your senior leadership team are your partners and first line of collaboration; leverage and trust them. Get commitment and buy-in from your team to achieve the big life-changing wins. Loyalty is earned through listening. Blind spots can be addressed and eliminated through feedback flows.

Secret #11: Paid ads are not the "easy button." Create your playbook, using this chapter's example modified for your company. Marketing is a full suite of brand building, demand generation, and messaging with your ideal prospects; hire your internal champion, test small, and scale with real insights, not impressions.

Secret #12: Don't delay when it's time to hire. Move fast, empower fully, and get out of the way. Waiting too long to bring in the right person will cost you time, traction, and trust. Your gut already knows what the role needs. Do it! Hire. Delegate. And let them run. Smart CEOs don't just build teams; they also trust them to deliver.

Secret #13: Do not ever hire a candidate on a "gut feeling" on the spot. Vet them properly through the hiring process that integrates and maps core competencies of the individual and the company. Adapt my eight-step framework to your company and make it happen. Your A-team starts here.

Secret #14: Great CEOs coach. But elite CEOs turn leadership development into a KPI. Assign each senior leader the responsibility and accountability to grow their teams. Make growth visible, measurable, and celebrated. Top CEOs don't just say, "our people are our greatest asset" because they visually prove it on an ongoing basis.

Secret #15: Never hire a VP of Sales before you've built a repeatable sales process. Your first sales hire should be a doer: someone who can prospect, pitch, and close; build demand first; then scale with leadership.

Secret #16: Motivation is personal. Don't assume cash moves everyone. As CEO, your job is to learn what drives each team, build trust with integrity, and lead with empathy. A wheelbarrow of cash can't buy trust, but it can shatter it.

Secret #17: The best CEOs don't do it all. They build teams they trust, set clear expectations, and delegate with discipline. Delegation is not giving up control. It's how you scale leadership.

Secret #18: Do not hire ahead of revenue. Hire based on revenue. Growth must be managed carefully, and scaling too fast can lead to setbacks that take years to recover from. But, with the right mindset, a willingness to make difficult and painful decisions, and a focus on recovery, it's possible to bounce back and build a stronger company for the future.

Secret #19: Your decision process is your CEO operating system. If you don't define it, it will define you. The best CEOs lead with clarity, not ambiguity, with every choice. They lead from the front. Lead with confidence, not chaos. Lead with decisions, not delays.

Secret #20: Your sales pipeline is not a fire drill; it's a daily discipline! As CEO, you should never take your eyeballs off revenue generation! It's your company lifeblood that drives all other decisions. There is never a time when you should let your guard down. Be prepared and accountable, and lead with confidence and power!

Secret #21: The best CEOs are not gut-driven or data driven, they are decision-driven! Make it a habit to test your instincts against primary information and data. Then you can make the call with confidence and power. Seat-of-the-pants decision-making is for amateurs, not top-notch CEOs.

Secret #22: Delaying a decision isn't always the worst choice. But doing so without transparency, prioritization, and a clear end point *is*. CEOs must learn to act with confidence, even when all the data isn't in. The job isn't just to make the right decision, it's also to make the decision right. That is leading with confidence and power.

Secret #23: Never give up full signature authority. If you do delegate, create a real-time method to know how every dollar was spent as well as where and for what. You, as CEO, are accountable.

Secret #24: Lead with integrity. Be open, honest, ethical, and accountable. There is no easy button. Execution matters. Trust matters. Truth Matters.

Elizabeth Holmes's downfall reminds us that your first responsibility as a CEO is to lead with integrity. There is a mini-series dedicated to it.

Secret #25: Silence isn't neutral; it's permission. When you see something wrong and say nothing, you've made a choice. You've told your team what you're willing to tolerate.

Leadership means doing the uncomfortable thing when everyone else stays quiet. Your team watches how you handle tough moments. That's when trust is built or broken

Don't flinch. Don't freeze. Do what's right. Every time.

Secret #26: Trust is hard to earn and easy to lose. Decisions made without transparency and integrity can have long-lasting consequences that impact not only the organization's performance but also its people, reputation, and future viability.

Secret #27: Don't postpone the inevitable. Trust your data backed instincts, make the difficult decision, and prevent greater problems from happening tomorrow.

Secret #28: Vision is powerful, but leadership sustains it and, in this case, changes the world!

Secret #29: A great cofounder multiplies your momentum. The wrong one multiplies your mistakes. Follow a process to vet and 100% align with your selected cofounder. Pick a cofounder like you're picking a spouse because, in some ways, it's harder to unwind.

Secret #30: Trust is earned. Verification is required. Startup CEOs must protect their company with contracts, controls, and clear decision rights, because one misstep can cost everything you've built. Remember this when selecting a cofounder.

Secret #31: Never split 50/50 with your cofounder. You are the CEO. Own the role, set the direction, and structure equity so that control and decision rights remain clear and undisputed.

Secret #32: You negotiate more than you think: equity splits, investor terms, and your title. Every "yes" or "no" either gives you power or gives it away. If you're not negotiating, you're being negotiated.

Secret #33: As a startup CEO, you own the capitalization table and all legal and financial agreements of the company. Even if you delegate, you are accountable. Verify every contract, capitalization table, option grant, and termination personally. Manage your capitalization table like your company depends on it, because it does! If it's messy, your business will be, too. Know every line, every share, and every agreement, because your investors will. Details matter!

Secret #34: Great partnerships don't happen by accident. Do the work. Ask the hard questions. Only move forward when values, vision, and trust are fully aligned, because getting it wrong can cost you everything.

Secret #35: The best CEOs aren't the smartest in the room, they're the ones who learn the fastest, reflect continuously, and act rapidly when it's necessary. These are the critical success factors to stay ahead of your company's growth curve and the reason your team will believe in you and your confidence.

Secret #36: Confidence isn't luck. It's earned in the daily grind and in every hard call, every missed shot you own, every lesson you don't dodge. Stack those wins, own those losses, and you'll carry a presence no title can give you. That's the power people follow.

Secret #37: Turn this Summary of Secrets into your reference guide. Print it, laminate it, and refer to it when you need start to feel the heat and need a refresher!

Conclusion

There you have it. Thirty-seven impact-filled chapters and secrets that will become your personalized decision frameworks, daily disciplines, and guide to success. You can and will lead with confidence and power as you perfect your leadership skills to handle anything that arises while keeping your calm and setting crystal clear expectations.

Appendix A

The Founder and First-Time CEO Confidence Weekly Checklist

This is your CEO dashboard. Like a pilot's dashboard, it shows all measurements in real time across your business.

To provide you an easy-to-read color-coded and scoring guide, use this:

Scoring guide:

- **Green** – A clear yes. You're on track.

- **Yellow** – Mostly yes. Needs a closer look.

- **Red** – No, or not sure. Fix this before anything else.

Check yourself every week. Reds get top priority until they turn green.

---

1. Vision & Strategy Confidence

"Do I know exactly where we're going and how we'll get there?"

- **Vision Clarity:** Can I explain our "why" in 30 seconds?

- **Team Alignment:** Can every team member name our mission and top 3 priorities?

- **Market Proof:** Have I spoken with at least 10 potential or current customers in the last month?

- **Problem-Solution-Fit:** Can I prove the problem exists and that our solution works? Do current customers and prospects agree?

- **Plan B Ready:** Do I have a backup plan if Plan A fails?

* * * **Red Flag:** If you can't clearly explain the "why," neither can your team.

---

2. Cofounder & Team Confidence

"Is my leadership team aligned, accountable, and protected?"

- **Roles Clear:** Everyone knows exactly what they own, with KPIs or scorecards in place.

- **Equity in Writing:** All equity splits and vesting schedules documented and signed off by legal.

- **Decision Rules:** A written process for how decisions are made and how deadlocks are broken.

- **Wrong Fit Removal:** Systems in place to quickly address poor performance or culture fit.

- **Core Values Lived:** Our 3–5 core values are visible in daily behavior, not just posters.

*** **Red Flag:** Cofounder disputes end more startup ideas than bad ideas. Lock this down early.

---

3. Legal & Financial Foundation

"Is the business built on solid ground?"

- **Clean Cap Table:** All shares issued and documented by legal.

- **IP Secured:** All intellectual property is assigned to the company, and patents filed or issued.

- **Trusted Advisors:** Startup-savvy attorney and accountant on call (fractional is fine).

- **Financial Systems:** Company accounts, credit cards, revenue recognition, and accounting processes in place.

- **Compliance Current:** Filings, taxes, and regulatory requirements up-to-date.

*** **Red Flag:** Legal mistakes cost more to fix than to prevent.

---

4. Fundraising & Investor Confidence

"Do I control the company's financial future?"

- **Runway Known:** I know exactly how much cash we have and how long it will last.

- **Burn Rate Tracked:** Spending forecasted at least 12–18 months ahead.

- **Investor Fit:** Every investor is vetted for experience, alignment, and value-add.

- **Update Rhythm:** Regular, scheduled investor updates (monthly or quarterly).

- **Next Round Plan:** Clear on timing, target valuation, and required metrics.

*** **Red Flag:** Running out of cash is the #1 startup killer.

---

5. Product & Customer Confidence

"Are we building something people will pay for and keep using?"

- **Customer Contact:** I talk to customers every week.

- **Feedback Loop:** Insights reach the product teams within 48 hours.

- **Roadmap Set:** Next 90 days of priorities are clear and communicated.

- **MVP Focus:** We're building what's needed now, not chasing "perfect."

- **Key Metrics:** We track retention, engagement, and satisfaction.

*** **Red Flag:** Build in isolation, and you'll miss the mark.

---

6. Revenue Engine Confidence

"Can I predictably generate and grow revenue?"

- **Pipeline Clear:** I know which deals will close in the next 90 days.

- **Sales Process:** Documented, repeatable steps from lead to close.

- **Founder-Led Sales:** I still handle top-tier opportunities.

- **Pricing Strength:** Our pricing is tested, defensible, and profitable.

- **Forecast Accuracy:** I can predict revenue within 20% each month.

***Red Flag:** Revenue is oxygen. Without it, nothing else matters.

---

7. Leadership & Culture Confidence

"Am I building a company people want to work for?"

- **Coaching First:** I develop people, not just manage tasks.

- **Celebrate Wins:** Weekly recognition, big or small.

- **Learn from Losses:** Post-mortems focus on lessons, not blame.

- **Values in Action:** Core values shape daily decisions.

- **Culture Health:** I measure and monitor engagement and satisfaction.

***Red Flag:** Bad culture spreads faster than good culture.

---

8. Personal CEO Confidence

"Am I growing as fast as my company needs me to?"

- **Strategic Time:** I block time for thinking and reflecting, not just doing.

- **Outside Input:** I have advisors, mentors, and/or peer groups I lean on.

- **Learning Captured:** I document key lessons and decisions.

- **Health Check:** My work-life balance is sustainable.

- **Brand Building:** I grow my personal and company visibility.

***Red Flag: If you stop growing, so will your company.

Weekly Scoring

Count your colors:

- **Green (8 - 7):** Strong position - keep momentum.

- **Yellow (6 - 4):** Solid but address the weak spots.

- **Red (3 - 0):** Urgent focus needed. Fix the top three now.

Track trends monthly and aim for steady improvement.

The 15-Minute Founder Fitness Test

Quick gut check:

1. Do I have at least 12 months of runway?

2. Can my team name our top three priorities?

3. Did I talk to a customer this week?

4. Is my cap table clean and documented?

5. Do I know what revenue will close next month?

5/5: You're ready to scale.

3 - 4/5: Patch the gaps now.

0 - 2/5: Stop and fix the foundation.

When You're Overwhelmed:

- Pick one red item and handle it today.
- Remember: every founder feels this way at some point.
- Call your mentor or advisor.

When You're Confident:

- Use the momentum to tackle bigger challenges.
- Help another founder.
- Write down what's working so you can repeat it.

When You're Stuck:

- Revisit your mission.
- Talk to a customer.
- Take a break. Clarity often comes in the quiet.

Final Word: Confidence comes from preparation. This checklist is your preparation system. Use it weekly. Fix what's broken. Build on what works. And lead like the CEO you set out to be.

Final Note from the Author

This book is filled with real stories from real CEOs. Real scars. Real lessons. If you've made it here, I hope you're walking away with one thing: **you are not alone, but you are responsible.**

CEOs who succeed are not mistake-free, but they are mistake-aware. They're learners, builders, and reflectors. They fail forward, adapt faster, and lead from a place of intention, not reaction.

And you can, too.

Let this be your pivot point. Let this be your next decision. Learn, reflect, and lead again.

You've got this.

There are several checklists, frameworks, and roadmaps in this book. Now that you have completed it, you can email me at bill@billmillertheCEOguy.com with the subject line: "Send me everything from 37 Secrets" and I will respond with either a link to all content or email them to the email address you provide.

Happy CEOing!

—Bill

About the Author

Bill Miller has been in the technology field for over 50 years. Over the past 35 years, Bill worked directly for some of the rookie CEOs featured in this book. His roles reporting to these rookies included Vice President of Marketing, Vice President of Product Management, Vice President of Product Management and Marketing, Vice President of Strategic Planning and Alliance Management, Vice President and General Manager of Broadband Services, Vice President of Operations, and Chief Operating Officer. He has been a blogger for ZDNet, TMCNet, BlogSpot, and for several companies.

Bill is a content advisor for "The Cloud Voice Alliance" where he hosts "The CEO Success Story" events. He has moderated "The CEO Insights Panel" at ITEXPO/Tech-Supershow annually since 2021 and author's "The CEO Insights Blog on TMCNet."

Bill founded Beelinebill Consulting in 2011, and he formed the parent company, Beelinebill Enterprises as well as Beelinebill Publishing in 2020.

Bill has been a speaker at dozens of conferences in networking, VoIP, unified communications, and collaboration markets. Today, he is an executive advisor and consultant on special projects.

- You can contact Bill by searching for @beelinebill or by emailing him.

- You can find Bill's CEO Success Story interviews and CEO Insights Panel videos on his YouTube channel.

Thank you for purchasing the book! We hope you enjoy it and benefit from the secrets and stories Bill and all guest CEOs have shared.

What's Next?

Love this book? Don't forget to leave a review!

Every review matters, and it matters a *lot!*

Head over to Amazon or wherever you purchased this book to leave an honest review.

If you felt the book did not meet your expectations, please email me and let me know why with your feedback so I can improve it in an update.

My links: https://linktr.ee/beelinebill

Thank you.